BUILT-IN FURNITURE FOR THE HOME

CHRIS GLEASON

POPULAR WOODWORKING BOOKS
CINCINNATI, OHIO
www.popularwoodworking.com

READ THIS IMPORTANT SAFETY NOTICE

To prevent accidents, keep safety in mind while you work. Use the safety guards installed on power equipment; they are for your protection. When working on power equipment, keep fingers away from saw blades, wear safety goggles to prevent injuries from flying wood chips and sawdust, wear hearing protection and consider installing a dust vacuum to reduce the amount of airborne sawdust in your woodshop. Don't wear loose clothing, such as neckties or shirts with loose sleeves, or jewelry, such as rings, necklaces or bracelets, when working on power equipment. Tie back long hair to prevent it from getting caught in your equipment. People who are sensitive to certain chemicals should check the chemical content of any product before using it. The authors and editors who compiled this book have tried to make the contents as accurate and correct as possible. Plans, illustrations, photographs and text have been carefully checked. All instructions, plans and projects should be carefully read, studied and understood before beginning construction. Due to the variability of local conditions, construction materials, skill levels, etc., neither the author nor Popular Woodworking Books assumes any responsibility for any accidents, injuries, damages or other losses incurred resulting from the material presented in this book. Prices listed for supplies and equipment were current at the time of publication and are subject to change.

METRIC CONVERSION CHART

to convert	to	multiply by
Inches	Centimeters	2.54
Centimeters	Inches	0.4
Feet	Centimeters	30.5
Centimeters	Feet	0.03
Yards	Meters	0.9
Meters	Yards	1.1

BUILT-IN FURNITURE FOR THE HOME. Copyright © 2008 by Christopher Gleason. Printed and bound in China. All rights reserved. No part of this book may be reproduced in any form or by any electronic or mechanical means including information storage and retrieval systems without permission in writing from the publisher, except by a reviewer, who may quote brief passages in a review. Published by Popular Woodworking Books, an imprint of F+W Publications, Inc., 4700 East Galbraith Road, Cincinnati, Ohio, 45236. First edition.

Distributed in Canada by Fraser Direct
100 Armstrong Avenue
Georgetown, Ontario L7G 5S4
Canada

Distributed in the U.K. and Europe by David & Charles
Brunel House
Newton Abbot
Devon TQ12 4PU
England
Tel: (+44) 1626 323200
Fax: (+44) 1626 323319
E-mail: postmaster@davidandcharles.co.uk

Distributed in Australia by Capricorn Link
P.O. Box 704
Windsor, NSW 2756
Australia

Visit our Web site at www.popularwoodworking.com or our consumer Web site at www.fwbookstore.com for information on more resources for woodworkers and other arts and crafts projects.

Other fine Popular Woodworking Books are available from your local bookstore or direct from the publisher.

12   11   10   09   08   5   4   3   2   1

Library of Congress Cataloging-in-Publication Data

Gleason, Chris, 1973-
  Built-in furniture for the home / by Chris Gleason.-- 1st ed.
    p. cm.
  Includes index.
  ISBN-13: 978-1-55870-831-0 (hardcover : alk. paper)
  ISBN-10: 1-55870-831-6 (hardcover : alk. paper)
  1. Built-in furniture. 2. Cabinetwork. 3. Shelving (Furniture) 4. Storage in the home. I. Title.
  TT197.5.B8G58 2008
  684.1'6--dc22

                                          2007051172

ACQUISITIONS EDITOR: David Thiel
SENIOR EDITOR: Jim Stack
DESIGNER: Brian Roeth
PRODUCTION COORDINATOR: Mark Griffin
PHOTOGRAPHER: Chris Gleason
CHAPTER OPENERS PHOTOGRAPHER: Paul Richer

about the author

Chris Gleason has owned and operated Gleason Woodworking Studio for nearly a decade. A self-taught craftsman, he specializes in contemporary furniture and built-in cabinetry. He is particularly inspired by mid-century Danish modern designs.

With a degree in French from Vassar College, in Poughkeepsie, New York, Chris had the opportunity to live and study abroad for a year in Switzerland. The mountain influence must have grabbed hold, as he now makes his home in Salt Lake City, Utah where he mountain bikes and skis as much as possible. He is also an enthusiastic old-time banjo and fiddle player.

acknowledgements

This book is built around a series of projects that I completed for my clients during the past year. Without their patience, cooperation and flexibility, this book never would have become a reality.

I also would like to thank Paul Richer, a talented and very busy photographer who somehow manages to find time to take the full-page beauty shots. He is a great problem-solver and a true professional.

To Jim Stack and David Thiel: Thanks again for giving me the opportunity to write this book and for all of your efforts in bringing it into its finished state. It is a joy and an honor to collaborate with you both.

My loving wife Michele also deserves a mention here for her never-ending encouragement and support.

contents

the many advantages of built-in furniture

Like most woodworkers, I love to build free-standing furniture. It is deeply satisfying to create a nice product that I can deliver to someone's home and immediately enjoy with no fuss and no mess. But, for as much as I enjoy the relative simplicity of this kind of process, I have found that it is hard to match the type of excitement and creative opportunity that larger-scale projects offer. Instead of building a piece of furniture for a room, you're taking it to the next level and building the room itself. And even though this creates a whole new set of challenges, the possibilities are usually just too good to turn down. This book is dedicated to helping you to develop and execute the big-design concepts that inspire you so that you can reshape entire rooms in efficient and enjoyable ways.

Aside from the fun factor, there are a number of notable reasons to undertake built-in projects. Great built-ins can:

ADD VALUE TO A PROPERTY You can leverage the skills and tools you already have by contributing your time and creativity. For only the cost of materials, you can add value to a property that you will enjoy for years to come, or you can sell the place and possibly reap a significant financial gain.

ADD CHARACTER Few elements can help to define the character of a room like built-ins. A formerly empty room can be transformed into a bona fide Arts & Crafts style den with the installation of a well-conceived fireplace mantle and some built-in bookshelves.

ADD STORAGE AND DISPLAY SPACE Who doesn't need more storage? Or maybe you'd like to show off a collection that you're proud of — the sky's the limit here.

ENHANCE THE USEFULNESS OF A SPACE Adding a home office area, or maybe even just a small nook in the kitchen for a laptop computer, can make it easier to get some work done, surf the internet or pay bills.

IMPROVE YOUR ENJOYMENT OF A SPACE You can put a television just about anywhere, but relaxing with family and friends in front of a wall-unit that has been custom designed for your entertainment needs sounds like more fun, doesn't it?

GOOD DESIGN IS IN THE DETAILS

I've heard it said that a kitchen is more than a bunch of cabinets that happen to be in the same place at the same time, and I think this same concept needs to be applied to built-in furniture. A nice built-in bookcase, for example, is more than a simple box that holds books. It makes optimal use of its intended space, and it can be a key component in helping to define the style and feel of the room. Good design starts with a great overall game plan and then proceeds consistently so that all of the small details add up to create exactly the right finished product.

Designing good built-in furniture demands that you precisely define what you're trying to do. If you're working in a 1920's bungalow, and you'd like to put in a set of Arts & Crafts style bookcases, a critical early step in the process will be to brush up on the details that help define that style. What sorts of materials, finishes, proportions, joinery, etc. will you decide to use? If you'd like glass doors, for example, what details in the door construction will make them look like they belong to that style? Are there particular moulding profiles that you should or shouldn't integrate into the design? Nowadays, the internet makes this process relatively quick and easy, but I also like to visit the library because it is nice to have a bunch of good books around the house when I'm doing a project like this — I can thumb through them at odd moments, and, I think, it helps me to get a handle on the particulars of a given project. This type of research is essential if you're trying to adhere to a historic style, and even if you're not, I think it is one of the best ways to build up a repertoire of ideas that you can draw on in future projects.

Now, it may be the case that you'll open a home design magazine and find your ideal project right there. In that case, you'll be starting out with a good deal of the design work taken care of. But, you'll still be faced with the challenge of adapting someone else's design to your unique home, and there will certainly be some head scratching involved. Then there's the question of how to execute the project so that it goes smoothly and with a minimum of fuss. No matter where you're starting out, the goal of this book is to provide useful information about developing a design concept into reality. Each of the projects is a case-study that breaks down a general idea into a series of steps that come together to create an efficient installation process and a great final product.

planning

Good measurements lead to good installations

T he planning process begins by amassing a lot of ideas about what you'd like to do. I think of this as "gathering the troops", and I find myself printing out pictures from favorite my Web sites, bookmarking magazines, tearing pages out of home furnishings catalogs and photocopying pictures from other sources I have at my disposal. This stage of the process is a lot of fun, and it is useful because the odds are good you will have other people involved (fam-

ily members and friends). This will help you to explain to them what you have in mind. Quick sketches can also be useful at this stage of the game.

Once you have some good ideas of how the finished product might look, I recommend taking accurate site measurements. If you're working in an unfinished space (i.e. a new or remodeled part of the house), I like to wait until the drywall is in place, but if time is of the essence you can always add the thickness of the drywall into the design and then plan for fillers or other ways of dealing with any discrepancies that may occur. Be forewarned — it can be shocking to see how much measurements change when drywall goes up.

A good site measurement, in any case, should be as accurate as possible — I take my time and have an assistant hold the other end of the tape if need be. I also bring along a 6' level so I can evaluate how straight the walls, floors and ceiling are. It is good to be aware early on if there are any radically sloping wall surfaces, because you can plan your construction to minimize the appearance of these defects easily.

This is also a good time to observe and record any other relevant information about the room. Details such as the position of electrical outlets may become critical later on. If an outlet falls on the inside of a cabinet, you can cut out the back of the cabinet and access it that way, and you're also in good shape if the outlet falls outside the cabinet, but what do you do when the edge of a cabinet — the cabinet that you've labored on and would like to install — lands smack in the middle of the outlet? Something will have to give, and it may not be cheap, easy or pleasant. This kind of headache is easy to avoid by paying close attention early on. For some of us, this kind of lesson has to be learned the hard way, but hopefully I can convince you to be careful and get it right the first time. I make sure to carefully note the position and size of baseboard mouldings, door casings, windows, plumbing fixtures, heating ducts and anything else that might get in the way or be a factor in how I design the components I'll be installing there.

Once I have the basic measurements of the space, I draw the project to scale. This can be an interesting phase of the design work, because details of the project that may have been a bit hazy beforehand can be worked out now. For example, sometimes

The plumbing shown here had to be rerouted through the base and still allow for the HVAC vent in the base. Planning ahead made this a part of the install, not a problem.

An electrical box exiting at the center of a cabinet is better than dead-on a cabinet side.

Anticipating on-the-job "adjustments" lets you plan ahead to have the proper tools on the job site.

it is hard to be clear on the proportions of the various components until you see the entire design represented in the same scale. I've been humbled more than once by realizing that the dimensions that I was "absolutely sure about" didn't look quite right once I had a finished drawing in front of me. Fortunately, making changes on paper doesn't cost much in time or materials.

Drawings don't need to be works of art and they don't need to take a lot of time, but they do need to convey an accurate sense of scale. A lot of people like to use graph paper for this purpose. If you're using blank paper, I recommend getting an architect's ruler, which makes it easy to draw using different scales. If you're into computers, there is a lot of reasonably priced software available — the appendix of this book will point out a few you might want to know about. In the end, your method of creating drawings comes down to personal preference. I am entrenched in the paper-and-pencil habit, but I have a great piece of software that I can use to draft an entire kitchen in just a few hours. This same software can rotate the project so you can see it from all angles — and that makes for an impressive presentation. I don't use it all the time, but it is a free program and it is nice to have on the hard drive when I want it. Again, you'll find more information on this in the appendix.

Each of the projects contained in the following chapters will describe the quirks of the various job sites. I'd like to present a list of universal rules-of-thumb that can be integrated into the way you think about job sites.

PLANNING RULES OF THUMB

Assume the floors aren't level. I am optimistic by nature, but I've learned to plan ahead and arrive ready to deal with uneven walls and out-of-level floors and ceil-

Level floor? Only if you're lucky!

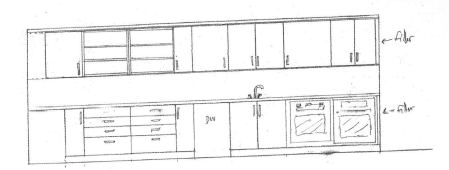

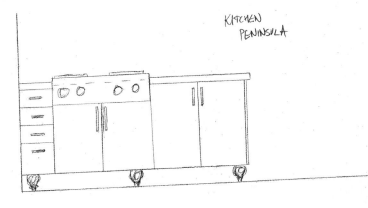

KITCHEN PENINSULA

ings. Knowing how to deal with these common challenges is essential. Filler strips, and over-sized trim pieces can help hide gaps and discrepancies — so be ready to implement them into the design.

Give yourself something to adjust with. If you have a 54"-wide opening, don't build two 27"-wide cabinets and figure that you'll get them in there somehow. Learning to scribe trim for an exact fit can be tricky, but I'll break it down into a series of very manageable and useful steps.

Consider the approach. When you perform your site measurement, I recommend taking a few minutes to consider the job site as a whole — what is the access like? Are there any tight corners you'll need to turn to get in? Stairways? Narrow doorways? Only once have I built a cabinet that was too big to get into a client's house. I will never do it again. I did not enjoy taking it apart in their driveway and re-assembling inside.

Design with the installation in mind. I assume the worst — that my delivery buddies will be off skiing and that I might need to do an entire installation myself. This puts me into the mindset of designing components in manageable sizes. This is less taxing on the back — and less stressful in general. Think ahead about installing wall cabinets. For example, I'd rather put up three small cabinets than one big, heavy cabinet that would be hard to lift and hold in position while it is being secured. Job sites can be stressful enough, so you'll be glad you simplified the process wherever possible. A series of smaller cabinets are also easier to move around the shop and work on than one monstrous one that will require a rental truck to get it down the road.

If you know that it's going to be just you doing the installation work, you can plan ahead to make things go easier. These jacks will let you hold an upper cabinet at an easily adjustable height while you screw the cabinet to the wall.

Nothing makes you feel better than knowing that the pieces all fit together. I'd rather know that before I'm on the job site. A dry run in the shop saves a lot of headaches.

Some problems are best solved by avoiding them. I have a nice crown moulding in my dining room and I didn't want to cover it up with the built-in bookshelves that I'd been planning for that wall. My solution was to lower the bookcases 12" from the ceiling. This was critical because the crown moulding is an important period detail throughout the downstairs of our Victorian-era home. The same technique might be used in a room where a ceiling is out of level. Rather than trying to figure out how to run crown moulding between the cabinets and the ceiling — there is no perfect solution here — you can avoid what would otherwise be a difficult situation.

With the right planning, you'll be able to transform a simple sketch into a beautiful built-in project.

fireplace surround with shelving

THIS FIREPLACE SURROUND is one of the first things you see when you come in the front door, so it is a great focal point for the room. The overall character of the house is transitional in nature — not too modern, but not particularly old-fashioned — this guided our design process and materials choices. We decided on a mix of concealed storage (in the bins) and display space on the bookshelves and the mantle top. We decided on 52" as the ideal height for the mantle, we wanted it to be high enough to be stately, but not out of scale with the 8' ceilings.

Rather than positioning everything along one plane, we built components of varying depths. This makes the layout more interesting and allowed us to address a few

practical concerns — the bins needed to be at least 12" deep for seating. We decided the mantel should 10" deep, the bookcases 8" deep and the trim panel above the firebox 5" deep. The existing firebox was surrounded by 6" tile. When working around a fireplace, it's a good idea to check your local building codes to see how much non-combustible material is required around the firebox.

CONSTRUCTION

Due to some inconsistencies in the size of the room, this design called for bookcases that weren't exactly the same width. The variation in the size of the bookcases wouldn't be readily noticeable, but it would allow me to keep consistent reveals between the bookcases and the window trim. This means that the bookcase bases needed to be sized accordingly, and I labeled them in order to make it easy to tell which was which on the job-site. This may seem unnecessary, but job-sites can be a little chaotic, so I try to eliminate potential snags whenever I can.

I used pocket screws to build the bookcases. The 1/4"-thick plywood backs were held in grooves that I ripped on my table saw with a dado blade. This will make for a nice clean look. Again, I labeled the parts so that I didn't mix them up during or after assembly. Once the bookcases were assembled, I set them up in the shop so I could see the project take shape. I feel that this makes the installation go more smoothly because I've practiced it before I get to the job site.

A panel made of 3/4" cherry plywood covered the area above the firebox and below the mantle. This added visual bulk and also contribut-

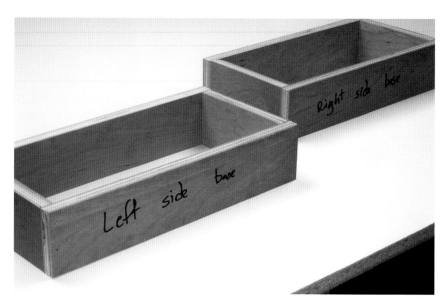

STEP 1 ■ I built the bases first and labeled them because they weren't the same size.

STEP 2 ■ I used my pocket-hole jig to drill holes in parts of the bookcases where they wouldn't show. Labeling these parts kept confusion to a minimum.

dealing with asymmetrical spaces

On this job, the features on the wall looked like they were symmetrical but they weren't. For example, the gap between the window and fireplace measured 3/4" larger on the left than the right, and, even more significantly, the gap between the window trim and the wall was 5" larger on the right side than on the left. Sometimes you can handle situations like this, but this time there wasn't much I could do. The reveals between the window trim and the bookcases needed to be uniform on both sides of the fireplace, so, to keep the reveals the same, I made the bookcase on the right 3/4" wider than the left bookcase. This difference isn't noticeable unless you know about it. The larger gap next to the adjacent walls, however, couldn't be remedied. The only solution I could come up with was to use a wider filler strip to fit where it was needed.

STEP 3 ※ Using a clamp kept the parts from wiggling out of alignment during assembly.

STEP 4 ※ Once they were assembled, I set up the bookcases in my shop to get a feel for how the project was shaping up.

ed to the built-in feel of the project. The panel had a strip secured to its bottom edge that returned to the wall. The panel was attached on site by screwing it directly to a pair of cleats that were glued and nailed to the bookcases during the in-shop mock up. I tacked it on with a couple of brad nails. The fasteners were hidden during the installation with some pieces of solid cherry trim.

The benches were boxes made of $3/4$" cherry plywood that were assembled with glue and nails. The exposed plywood edges were covered with edge-banding on the top and solid-cherry trim on the front.

I built up the mantle top with scrap wood so it measured 2"-thick. I then attached $2" \times 3/8"$ cherry trim to the front and sides using miter joints to keep the end grain hidden. I like to use blue painter's tape to hold pieces in place while the glue dries. The tape is easy to apply and it comes off without marring the surface of the wood.

STEP 5 ※ I attached a set of cleats to the sides of the bookcases so I could secure the front panel to the bookcases.

STEP 6 ※ The area above the firebox was trimmed with a panel. The panel also needed to be trimmed on its underside, so I attached a piece of cherry plywood to it, creating an L-shaped subassembly.

STEP 7 ■ A couple of brad nails held the panel temporarily in place during the mock up.

STEP 8 ■ The benches were made of ³/₄" plywood throughout.

STEP 9 ■ The mantle top was built up to be 1¹/₂" thick.

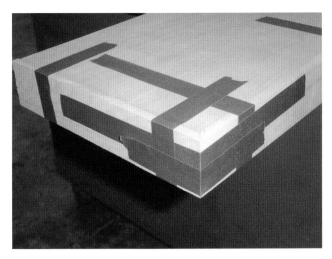

STEP 10 ■ The plywood edges of the mantle top were covered with 1/4"-thick cherry trim mitered at the corners. The trim was held in place with tape while the glue dried.

STEP 11 ■ The bookcases were fitted with face frames to give them some visual bulk. The face frames were joined with pocket screws on their back sides.

To bulk up the 3/4" plywood edges, I used 2"-wide face frame parts for the bookcases. I edged the floating shelves with the same material. Before the bookcases were trimmed out, they didn't look beefy enough, but the face frames made a difference.

Figuring out how to make the bench tops took a little head scratching. The design required "captured" ends on the benches, which is to say they butt directly against the wall and needed to be custom-fitted on site. I ended up making the bench tops slightly over-sized so they could trimmed as needed. I began with plywood rectangles that I ripped into a wider front part and a narrower back one. I then crosscut the front part on a table saw sled so that I had strips I could re-join to the back strip using biscuits

STEP 12 ■ The front edges of the shelves were beefed up with 2"-wide trim.

staying organized on the job site

I like to set up a simple command center with a pair of sawhorses and some scrap plywood to make a table where I can work etc. I also bring in everything at once (all tools and all components because it bugs me to interrupt my workflow once I'm up to speed). Also set up the various components on site so they're accessible... helps to feel organized. Not an attempt to mock anything up or problem-solve—just making things accessible and organized so that when I want them, I'm not disturbed by making a million trips back and forth to the van.

Once on site, I set all of the components to the side so they were easily accessible.

I like to set up a small work area when I'm doing site work. It's a lot easier to work at a convenient height when you can.

STEP 14 ▪ I used biscuits to reassemble the parts into a U-shape. The lid nestled neatly into the void in the middle.

and dominos. The grain matched up nicely and the top appeared to be made from one piece with a precisely cut out bench lid. Once the tops had been fit on-site, they were secured to the benches with cleats and screws.

STEP 13 ▪ The bench tops were complex. I wanted them to be cut from one piece of wood so the grain flowed evenly across their surfaces. This necessitated a special cutting sequence. First, I ripped off the back edge, then I crosscut the center section to separate the lid from the end piece.

INSTALLATION

I began the installation by laying out the bases and marking the walls to indicate the future positions of the cabinets — this helped me to quickly get the lay of the land and see how best to proceed. In this case, the hearthstone stood nearly 1/2" above the rest of the floor height. It was easy to identify this as the high point of the floor. I set the bookcase bases into position and shimmed them level. The right-hand base had to be shimmed higher to be level with the left-hand base, which illustrates an important concept: You need to raise all the components to the highest point to achieve a level

STEP 15 ▪ The job site was ready for the installation. The baseboards mouldings hadn't been installed yet, so I didn't have to bother removing them.

setting up shop, outside the shop

It is common sense that you won't bring the same tools every time, because no two projects are the same, and no two job sites are the same. And if you're working out of a home shop, then you might get lucky and already have most of the necessary items close at hand anyway. Here's a list of things that should cover most of the bases for you most of the time:

safety glasses

dust masks

shims

razor blades

compass/scribe

levels (6', 4', 2', 1')

tape measure

plans, notes and spec sheets for
    appliances, etc.

belt sander

jigsaw

miter saw

portable table saw

power planer

Dremel tool/Rototip

drill bits

countersinks

flexible drill extension (10")

hole saws and spade bits

masonry bits

brad nailer—self-contained or
    compressor driven

Sharpie

mechanical pencils

Allen wrenches

channel locks

needle-nosed pliers

rubber mallet

stud finder with working battery

utility knife

crescent wrench

a couple of quick-squeeze clamps

screws – 1/2", 3/4", 1", 1 1/4", 2", 2 1/2"
    and 3"

wall anchors such as toggle bolts, etc.

concrete anchors such as Tapcon screws and
    E-Z-Anchors

shop vacuum

colored nail filler putty or sticks

screw caps to match the project's materials

masking tape

double-sided tape

sandpaper– various grits

finishing products to match the project– i.e.
    lacquer, polyurethane, etc.

stain

paper towels and/or rags

drop cloth or builder's paper to
    protect floors

wood glue (type 1,2 or 3)

superglue with accelerator

construction adhesive

extension cords

step ladder, if needed

folding saw horses

template for drilling holes for door &
    drawer pulls

STEP 16 ■ I used a long level to level the bookcase bases. This required a few shims but nothing out of the ordinary.

STEP 17 ■ The bench bases were shimmed up as needed.

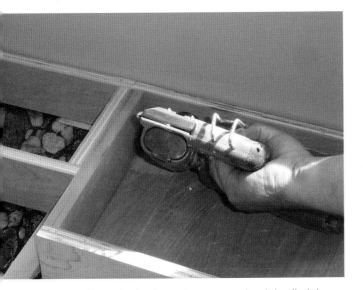

STEP 18 ■ Once the bookcase bases were level, I nailed the bench bases to them.

STEP 19 ■ You can see just how out-of-level the floors were in this corner of the room.

run. Phrased differently: It is harder to lower a cabinet base than shim it up. If it is absolutely necessary, you can shave down a base so the top stops at a particular height, but this isn't often needed.

Once the bookcase bases were in place, I sat the bench bases into place and nailed them to the bookcase bases. I then shimmed up their far ends so that everything read level. I took a photo to show the huge variation in the floor — it was put in just two weeks prior to my installation.

The moral of the story: Don't show up on a job site without shims!

Once I had leveled the bases, I sat the bookcases in place and secured them to the back wall, after which I installed the back panel. I nailed the back panel to the cleats on the sides of the bookcases, just as I had during my mock up, but this time I reinforced it with 2" screws. I trimmed it out with 2" trim strips. Out of habit, it was tempting to use miters here, but there are no miters any-

STEP 20 ▪ Installing the bookcases was simple — they dropped into place and I screwed them to the studs.

STEP 21 ▪ The front panel was screwed securely to the cleats on the bookcase.

STEP 22 ▪ The back wall was wavy.

where else in the project and the overall feel is rectilinear. In my judgement, angled cuts would have looked out of place so I went with butt joints.

The order of operations wasn't too critical from here. I decided to install the mantle top, which needed to be scribed to fit the back wall. To make the cut, I used a new blade (be sure to choose an appropriate blade for the material you're cutting). Note: This didn't apply here, but when I'm cutting across the grain of veneer ply, I score the cut line with an Exacto blade to minimize tearout.

Before I could secure the mantle top to the bookcases, I needed to finish off its bottom side with two layers of $1/4$" cherry ply (I should have used $1/2$"). I hadn't realized it that this was an issue until I executed my mockup, but this was important. It helped to bump up the mantle so it didn't hang too low and obscure the top of the bookcase trim.

The benches slipped easily into place, and I made sure to recheck them with levels so nothing shifted. They were then screwed to studs in the back wall and to the adjacent bookcases.

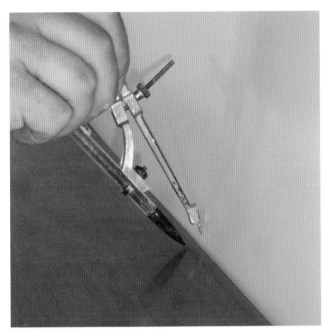

STEP 23 ■ I used a compass to transfer the irregular profile of the back wall to the mantle top. I trimmed away the excess and the top fit neatly.

STEP 24 ■ The edges of the front panel were trimmed to match the face frames. It was also a handy way of hiding the screw heads.

STEP 25 ■ Before I could secure the top, I needed to trim its underside.

STEP 26 ■ The final result.

STEP 27 ■ The benches also dropped right into place and were screwed to the studs in the back wall.

STEP 28 ■ To trim the bench tops to fit, I needed to make a template of the areas where they would be placed. I started by scribing a strip to fit against the back wall.

STEP 29 ■ I scribed a strip against the side of the bookcase and fastened it to the back strip.

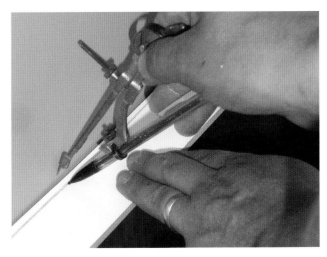

STEP 30 ■ No free lunch here — I had to scribe every side.

STEP 31 ■ I placed another strip across the front edge and finally had a finished template.

STEP 32 ■ By tracing the shape of the template directly onto the bench-top blank, I was able to create a nicely-fitting bench top.

On the right-hand side we stopped the bench cabinet shy of the outlet and vent. That solved the problem by avoiding it.

On the right-hand side I didn't use the filler. I had been planning to because there was an outlet we wanted to bring through to the front of the filler but I had to cut around that. I made sure not to attach the top of the bench so an electrician could come back, extend the wiring and hook up the outlet.

The bench tops were challenging because they had to be trimmed to fit into eccentrically-shaped openings — I needed to make templates. Prior to getting to the job site, I ripped a stack of 2"-wide strips of 1/4"-thick MDF. To fabricate the templates, I first set the back strip in place and scribed as needed. This isn't always neces-

sary — sometimes you'll be working with a nice flat wall — but I've had plenty of instances where all sides needed scribing. This was one of them. For the front edge, I let the template overhang 1/4" (my blank was deep enough to allow for this). Once the template was finished, I traced its shape onto my blank and jigsawed it to shape. I repeated the process for the other bench top.

The bench tops were attached to the benches with nails and construction adhesive. I reinforced the tops by adding cleats directly below them inside the bins.

The final step was trimming the toe kicks. This is usually straightforward, but in this case the floors were out of whack, so I ended up having to scribe nearly every piece of trim. I mitered the corners for a neater appearance.

home office

CREATING A HOME OFFICE from scratch is a satisfying accomplishment because it provides the opportunity to fully use a space. Whether you're surfing the internet, paying bills or sitting down to get some work done, it is a real luxury to have a space that is useful, comfortable and beautiful. And, when the furnishings blend into the architecture and décor of the room, so much the better.

This home office is located in a funky loft-style condominium, so we chose our materials accordingly: The major design element is the Baltic birch plywood. We left the edges exposed for a raw, industrial look. Originally an old warehouse, the concrete floors were cleaned and polished and they add tons of character, but there is a cost. They were out of level, so that posed a few challenges during the installation. The end result was great however — a built-in home office that fit neatly into the space and met my client's needs.

CONSTRUCTION

I built these cabinets with biscuits and their assembly
was straightforward. My clients loved the look of the
edges of the Baltic birch plywood, so we nailed the cabinet backs on to show this off. Note that the upper cabinets have painted backs. In order to get the neatest result
in the most efficient way, I painted the backs first and
then attached them once the paint was dry. This is much
easier than masking off the unpainted portions and trying
to paint the cabinet after assembly.

When installing drawer slides, sometimes it is just as
easy to flip the cabinet onto its side and then you don't
have to fight gravity or take the time to make a spacer.
The lower slide, as is often the case with this style of
undermount slide, sat directly on the cabinet bottom. I
needed to measure up and make a couple of marks to position the upper slide.

To avoid covering up the edge of the Baltic birch plywood, I planned for inset-style doors and drawer fronts.
To install the inset door, I held it in place with shims and
then reached through the top of the cabinet to screw the
hinges plates into place — a common sense approach
that has never failed me. Beware that inset doors can be
tricky to work with. Cabinet boxes that are square in the
shop can sometimes be tugged out of square on the job
site, so you may need to adjust the door's fit once the cabinet is installed. I like to use European-style 35mm hinges
because they can be adjusted
with the turn of a screw.

When it comes to attaching
the door and drawer pulls, if
I've only got a couple to attach,
I don't usually bother to make
or use a store-bought template.
In this case, there was only one
door, so I positioned the pull so it
looked nice and was set in evenly from the edge and drilled my
holes accordingly. The drawer
fronts were identical so I used
one as the template for the other.

I assembled the light valance
assembly with biscuits. Just to
play it safe, I left the valance 1"
too long and $^1/_2$" too deep so
that it could be trimmed on-site
if need be. This means that I'm
creating more work for myself

STEP 1 ■ I established a modern look for this project by leaving the edges exposed on the Baltic birch plywood.

STEP 2 ■ Whenever possible, I like to install drawer slides into a cabinet by tipping it onto
its side. This way you don't have to rip spacers to hold the slides in place.

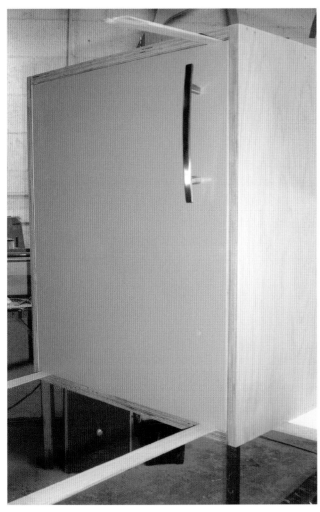

STEP 3 ■ Inset doors can be tricky to fit. I shim them all around to get an ¹/₈" gap on all sides, then I can just reach in from the top and screw the hinges plates onto the cabinet side. This is the easiest approach I've been able to come up with.

STEP 4 ■ 35mm hinges offer a range of adjustment in case it is required on site — and it probably will be.

STEP 5 ■ When I only have a couple of drawer pulls to mount, I don't take the time to make a template — I just set the pull in place and mark for a pair of corresponding holes.

STEP 6 ■ I used biscuits to assemble the light valance.

on the job site, but if I didn't leave myself the wiggle room and I needed it, I'd have a real problem on my hands.

The desktop is made of ³/₄" plywood that has a built-up edge to give it a beefier look. I also reinforced it with a series of stretchers that I glued and nailed to the underside. They will help stiffen the top and ensure that it sits evenly on my cabinets.

INSTALLATION

I always take a few minutes to refresh my memory about the unique space that I'll be working in. On busy job sites that involve a number of tradesmen, this is especially important because I sometimes find that things have changed significantly between the time when I made my initial

field measurements and the time I'm ready to install. For example, I usually start off looking for things like electrical outlets and heating vents that I'll have to deal with. I also keep an eye out for trim or mouldings that I'll need to remove or work around. I carry a level around the job site and reconnoiter a bit to see how level or out-of-level the walls and floors are so that I can plan accordingly. This job site will definitely provide some challenges!

Although there are exceptions to this rule, most of my built-in pieces have bases that can be set in place and adjusted to provide a level platform for the other components. In this case, the floors were out of level, so I knew I'd have a lot of shimming to do. I started by spacing the bases along the back wall. The adjacent (right-hand) wall

STEP 7 ■ The desktop needed to be built up on its underside with scrap plywood.

STEP 8 ■ When I first arrive on site, I take a minute to evaluate the potential challenges — in this case I needed to cut around a couple of outlets and a heating vent.

STEP 9 ■ I began the installation by setting the cabinet bases into their approximate positions.

STEP 10 ■ To make sure that the bases are level, I drew a level line across the back wall and measured down from it to the tops of the cabinet bases. The longest measurement indicated the lowest spot on the floor. The low spots needed to be shimmed up until they equaled the shortest measurements.

STEP 11 ⊠ I rechecked everything with a long level.

STEP 12 ⊠ I used a short *torpedo* level to confirm that the bases were level from front-to-back.

wasn't quite flat, so I needed to use a filler strip to accommodate this variation. I had a 3"-wide filler strip, so I bumped the cabinet out 1$^1/_2$" from the wall which provided plenty of room to trim the strip down.

I used my 7' level to draw a level line along the back wall. If the cabinets had run along the adjacent wall, I would've extended the line down that wall too. The height of this line isn't important — we're not trying to establish a desktop height or anything at this point — but it should be at a convenient working height. It's nice to have a helper to hold a long level like this.

To level the bases, I measured down from the line to the top of the cabinet bases and recorded the measurements. Understanding this phase is critical: I was looking for the smallest number, because it indicated the highest point of the floor. This is important because I could then shim up the lower spots until they measured the same as my smallest measurement. The back edges of my bases were then level. I then checked them from front-to-back using a smaller level. I needed to do a bit of shimming here, then I re-checked everything with my big level. You can't

STEP 13 ⊠ I set the right-hand cabinet into place, making sure to overhang it on the left-hand side of the base so that my $^1/_4$" toe kick trim would fit. I then screwed the cabinet to the studs in the back wall.

STEP 14 ■ The adjacent wall was uneven so I had to scribe a filler strip and insert it into the gap.

STEP 15 ■ I secured the filler strip with nails.

STEP 16 ■ To make the cutout in the back of the other base cabinet, I drew a vertical line representing the edge of the cabinet side and used it as a reference point to locate the outlet.

STEP 17 ■ I transferred these measurements to the cabinet back and made my cutout.

STEP 18 ■ The fit was just right.

STEP 19 ■ I made the desktop extra deep so that I had enough material to be able to trim off if necessary.

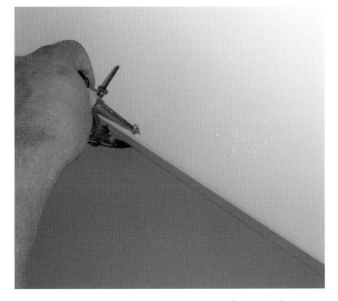

STEP 20 ■ I ran my compass against the wall to trace its profile onto the desktop. I cut away the excess with a jigsaw and created a nice fit.

STEP 21 ■ I screwed the desktop into place from below.

be too careful because this phase of the project sets the stage for everything else that will follow.

It is possible that checking the bases from front-to-back would reveal that they sloped too much toward the back. This wasn't the case for me here, but in such a situation, you'll need to raise the backs of the bases so the bases are level from front-to-back. Then you can adjust the front edge as need to compensate. If this sounds confusing, don't worry. Once you actually have the project in front of you, it will seem much less abstract, and even

though job sites are all different, this basic process will always work.

Once the bases were level, I screwed them to the studs in the wall.

Setting the base cabinets in place was straightforward because the bases were already level, so I screwed them to the studs. I needed to attach a filler strip to the right-hand side of the cabinet, however, which complicated things a bit. The filler strip started out as a rectangular piece of stock that I finished to match the other compo-

file storage

When it comes to file storage, you have a couple of options. You can purchase aftermarket file rails that will fit into a drawer that you've already built, or you can cut some file rails into a drawer as you build it. Aftermarket rails may look a bit more polished, which might be a consideration, and many of them will allow you to use a drawer of any width, which might come in handy. If you build drawers that you have sized for files, you can easily cut a rabbet along the top edge of an opposing pair of slides and let the files slide on the remaining ridge. I've done this on some cabinets that I've been using for a few years now and they seem to work—and last—just fine.

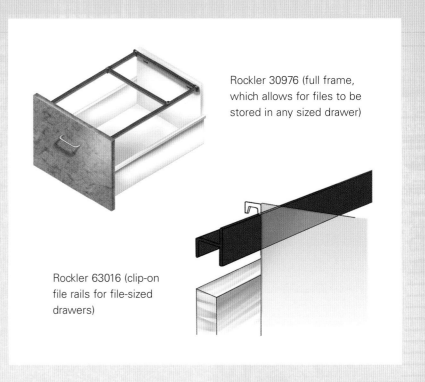

Rockler 30976 (full frame, which allows for files to be stored in any sized drawer)

Rockler 63016 (clip-on file rails for file-sized drawers)

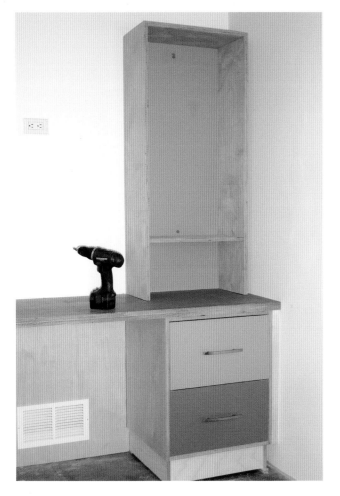

STEP 22 ▪ At right, because the desktop is level, the bookcase sat level and I was able to simply screw it to the studs.

STEP 23 ▪ A filler was also required here. You can easily see how out-of-plumb the wall was.

STEP 24 ▪ I set the left-hand bookcase into place and marked its location carefully so that I could drill a centered hole for the wiring grommet.

STEP 25 ▪ A 2¹/₂" hole saw did the job quickly and neatly.

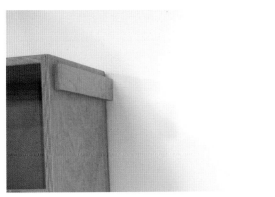

STEP 26 ▪ The light valance was supported by a pair of cleats attached to the bookcases.

nents. I held it up against the wall, used a compass to follow the profile of the wall and drew a pencil line on the filler. Once the excess was trimmed, my filler fit neatly against the wall. I then trimmed the other side of the filler by measuring the gap between the wall and the cabinet at the top and bottom of the spot where the filler was to be installed. I transferred these measurements to the filler strip and cut away the excess on that side. The filler then slid perfectly into place and I secured it with glue and nails. (More information on this process can be found on the included DVD).

The base cabinet on the left didn't need a filler strip, but I did have an electrical outlet that I had to cut around. We were glad to have it there, though, because it would

provide a concealed place for my client to plug in his computer and accessories.

I started the process by marking the wall where the cabinet would be placed. This gave me a line to measure from. The two questions are: How far up and how far over? This mantra guides me through every cutout that I make in situations like this. You need to measure from the base up to the bottom and top of the outlet. You also need to measure from the edge of the cabinet to the near and far sides of the outlet. I recorded these measurements on the wall since they would be covered up.

Before cutting with a jigsaw or RotoZip, check and re-check your measurements. Be sure that you're measuring from the correct side of the cabinet! I mention this

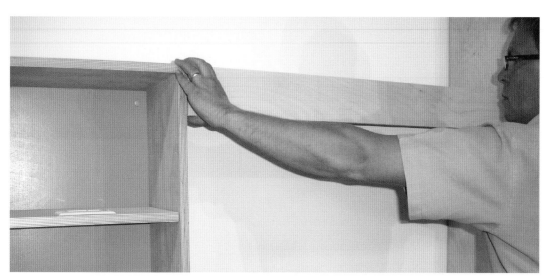

STEP 27 ■ I built the light valance extra long so I could trim it down to size.

STEP 28 ■ I constructed a template out of strips of scrap plywood to help me map out the space where the corkboard would sit.

because I've messed up before and needed to replace a cabinet back, which is not something I recommend if you're shooting for efficiency. Once the cutout is finished, you can screw the cabinet to the studs.

For a freestanding desk, we would just attach the desktop and call it a day — but not in this case. I wanted a precise fit between the desktop and the walls, but the back wall had a lot of irregularities, and the corner wasn't quite square either. When I have to scribe a long, narrow surface (like a countertop or desktop) into place, I start with the smaller side. Using my compass, I transferred the profile of the wall to the desktop and cut away the extra material. Once it fit nicely, I repeated the process on the long side. When I was finished, I attached the top to the cabinets from below.

The upper cabinets didn't require any leveling because the desktop was level. The right-hand cabinet needed to be set out 1½" from the wall to match the cabinet below it. I screwed it to the studs and installed a filler strip just like I did earlier.

Before setting the cabinet on the left-hand side, I needed to layout the location for the hole that I planned to drill to facilitate cord and cable routing. I set the cabinet into place and centered the hole.

With the hole drilled and the cabinet secured, I installed a pair of cleats that would support my light valance. The valance was trimmed to fit and screwed into place through the top and sides. This created a framed-in area on the back wall where I wanted to apply some cork. I made a template for this area just like I did for the back panel below the desk. I attached the cork to the drywall with contact adhesive and cut out around the outlet with a utility knife.

STEP 29 ▪ I set the template atop the cork and traced it to create a piece of cork that fit perfectly.

Our design called for a back panel that contributed to the built-in feel of the project. When I made the panel, I cut it slightly oversize so that it could be trimmed to fit onsite. I also didn't assume that a rectangular shape would fit perfectly, because in the real world, things aren't always square, flat and level. To accommodate a space that might not be perfectly regular, I used a simple technique to build a template which I then used to trace onto my panel blank. This technique is invaluable for fitting desktops, countertops and other things into oddly-shaped spaces.

Using scrap strips of $^1/_4$" material, I held the strips along the edges of the area where I needed to use the template. Using a compass, I transferred the profile of each surface onto the strips and cut away the excess. Labeling the strips is essential. Once the strips were all trimmed, I screwed them together to make a tightly-fitting "map" of the space. (This technique is demonstrated in detail on the DVD).

Once the blank was sized properly, I tested its fit and measured for the cutout for the heat vent. I transferred the

STEP 30 ▪ I attached the cork directly to the wall with contact adhesive.

measurements to the panel just like I did when I cut out for the electrical outlet.

Even with the out-of-level floors, trimming-out the cabinet bases went smoothly because I proceeded one piece at a time and made sure to label everything. I used baseboard trim that was extra wide so it could be trimmed down. I measured the height for each piece of trim at both ends of its length. This is important because some of the trim pieces tapered along their lengths as they followed the slope of the floor. I marked the measurements onto the trim, ripped them to the required width and marked the pieces for the miter joints. Miters provide a nice, clean finished look, and they didn't take much longer than simple butt joints would have. Once the pieces were cut and test-fitted, I glued them into place using a hot-melt polyurethane glue (Franklin's HiPurformer).

Early on in the process, I noted that the back wall wasn't exactly flat from top-to-bottom. This produced an uneven gap between the cabinet backs and the wall. There is no way to eliminate the gap, so concealing it is the best approach. I used some trim strips scribed to a nice fit against the wall and glued them into place. The baseboards also needed to be scribed to fit against the irregular profiles at the bottom of the cabinets. The overall look was nice and neat.

STEP 31 ▪ I used a utility knife to cut out around the outlet after the cork was in position.

STEP 32 ▪ Because the floors were so uneven, each piece of toe kick trim had to be custom-made. I labeled them to avoid mix-ups.

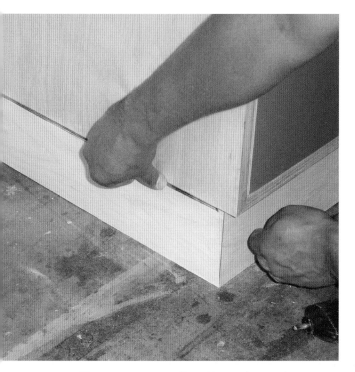

STEP 33 ▨ The corners were mitered to produce a nice, clean result.

STEP 34 ▨ The toe kick trim took a while but it was worth it—the project has a true built-in feel.

STEP 35 ▨ To cover the small gap at the back edge of the left-hand bookcase, I scribed a piece of trim and glued it in place.

STEP 36 ▨ I also had to scribe the baseboards.

project three

window surround with bench seat

THIS IS A NEAT PROJECT that can be varied in a lot of ways to suit almost any setting and décor. You could easily modify it for a more contemporary look by changing the materials and finishes — the actual techniques for the construction and installation will be applicable across the board. I think it illustrates how a few simple components — in this case a tall bookcase and a low bench — can be built into a home in such a way as to completely redefine the space. In this case, I used beadboard and a few ornate mouldings to create both the period look and the built-in feel that my client and I wanted.

This project also stands out because of its raised, furniture-style bases. They look great, but they did require a novel approach to get them installed correctly.

CONSTRUCTION

This project stands out largely because of its elegant furniture style bases. Because this project was to be painted, I built the bases out of pine. I attached the feet to the stretchers with Dominos, but you could use any number of joinery methods. Once the joints were all cut, I clamped up the bases and, while the glue dried, moved on to the cabinets.

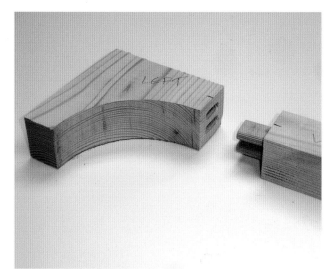

STEP 1 ▪ This project is unique because of its furniture-style base. I used domino fasteners to quickly create strong joints.

STEP 2 ▪ Labeling the parts helps keep confusion to a minimum.

STEP 3 ▪ As usual, I began mocking up the project as soon as possible.

MDF is an ideal material for painted projects because it is easy to work with and provides a nice uniform surface for a painted finish. The edges won't absorb paint evenly, however, so you need to cover them. This project called for 2"-wide face-frame trim. MDF doesn't hold screws particularly well, so I used biscuit joints on the corners. The backs were glued and screwed on. Where they joined the cabinet sides they were only exposed in a couple of areas and these could easily be covered up during the installation.

The bench top was built up to be 1½"-thick by screwing and gluing scrap MDF to the bottom side. I trimmed the edge with an embellished rope moulding. The top is made 1" longer and 1" deeper than necessary — this will provide enough wiggle room to allow it to be trimmed to fit on-site.

STEP 4 ■ The bench top was built up from ³/₄" MDF. I chose this material because it provides a stable, even surface for paint.

STEP 5 ■ The bench top was embellished with rope moulding on two sides and is mitered at the corner.

STEP 7 ▪ The job site before photo. An otherwise plain interior was about to be greatly improved.

STEP 6 ▪ With a coat of primer on it, the project started to visually come together.

STEP 8 ▪ I had to remove the baseboards before I could do anything else. I used a piece of sheet metal against the wall to protect the drywall as I removed the base (photo at left). The paint needed to be touched up below the cabinets because I was not planning to replace the baseboard there (photo above). Luckily the homeowners had saved some of the original paint.

STEP 9 ■ Even though there are two bases involved here, I treated them as one unit, using a level to check how they sat.

STEP 10 ■ It is important to check the front-to-back alignment at multiple points along the run of bases.

INSTALLATION

Site preparation was easy — I only had to remove the baseboards. While removing the baseboards, I used a scrap piece of tin to protect the wall from being damaged by my pry bar. I knew I wouldn't be putting the baseboards back along the entire length of the wall, so I touched up paint on the bottom edges where necessary.

Leveling the raised furniture-style bases requires a different approach than you would use with traditional cabinet bases. Instead of shimming everything up to the same height as the high spot, you need to remove material from the leg that sits over the high spot until the bases sit level. This may take a couple of tries.

I began by setting the bases into place and using a level to check out how they sat. They were perfectly level from side-to-side, but checking from front-to-back revealed a high spot in the back left corner. This had been noticeable to the eye, but further checking with a level at several positions along the length of the bases confirmed that the back corner was in fact $3/16"$ too high. I adjusted this by cutting $3/16"$ off of the back foot of the tall bookcase base. Once I repositioned the bases, they sat perfectly

STEP 11 ■ Ordinarily we would shim up bases up to meet the high spot, but with these furniture-style bases, shims would stand out. So, the pro-move was to cut off the extra material at the high spot.

STEP 12 ■ Once the bases sat level, they were screwed together. I then screwed the bases to the studs in the wall.

level, so I screwed them together and then screwed the whole assembly to the studs in the rear wall.

I placed the tall cabinet on the base and checked its position with a level. Because the base had already been leveled, the cabinet should also be plumb and level. Fortunately, this was the case, so I screwed it to the studs in the back wall.

To put up the beadboard wall paneling, I began by drawing a level line 40" from the floor. My plan called for beadboard to run 60" from left to right, which was too wide to cut from a single 48"-wide sheet. I knew that I would need to piece it together from multiple parts. I started on the left-hand side, measuring, cutting and installing one piece at a time. This was easy and produced a higher-quality result than cutting all the parts at once and hoping they would fit. I had to pay attention to aligning the joints properly so the beadboard pattern was consistent across the span. The beadboard was glued to the drywall with construction adhesive — the nails served mainly to hold the beadboard in place until the adhesive had set.

STEP 13 ■ After slipping the tall case onto the base, I used a level to check that the bookcase side was plumb. It was.

STEP 14 ■ The low bench dropped neatly into place and was attached to the bookcase and the wall.

STEP 15 ◾ I used a long level to draw a line at the spot where the beadboard would terminate.

Before I could set the final piece of beadboard into place, I needed to nail the baseboard on the right-hand side of the bench. The fit wasn't perfect, so it needed to be scribed and cut. To mark the baseboard, I set a compass to 1/4" wide (just slightly bigger than the widest part of the gap) and ran it up and down along the edge of the bench's base. This profile was then traced onto the baseboard, which I cut out with a jigsaw. Once the baseboard was in place, I measured for the final piece of beadboard.

The beadboard was capped off with a chair rail. To create a nice fit, I rabbeted the back edge of the chair rail on my table saw. This allowed me to neatly cover the top edge of the beadboard and it provided some wiggle room to make sure that the chair rail sat level even if the top edge of the beadboard didn't. The beadboard was finished off on the right-hand side with a shop-made moulding.

It was a good thing that I made the bench top extra wide and deep because the fit wasn't perfect out of the gate and it needed to be trimmed down. Using my compass, I scribed and cut the left-hand edge first, then I re-

STEP 16 ◾ Because the span of beadboard was wider than the 48"-wide sheets I had to work with, I knew I would have some seams. I decided to put it up in sections, with the divisions falling wherever it was convenient. It seemed like common sense to run a long rectangle up the left-hand edge.

STEP 17 ▪ I ran another rectangular piece of beadboard below the window. A bit of caulk covered up the seam perfectly.

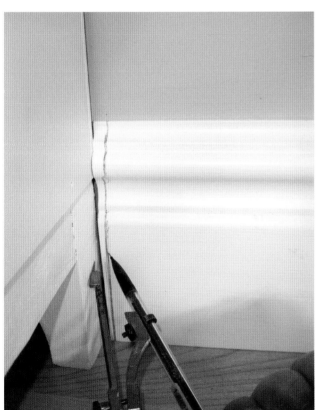

STEP 18 ▪ Before I could finish installing the beadboard, I needed to install the baseboards. To get a clean fit, I scribed the end of the baseboard to the cabinet's base.

STEP 19 ▪ With the baseboard in place, I marked out a vertical line to delineate the right-hand edge of the area to be covered in beadboard.

STEP 20 ■ Voilà! Using beadboard on the wall and the cabinet backs gives it a built-in look and feel.

peated the process on the back side. As a rule of thumb, I find it makes sense to scribe the short edge first, then the long edge. (If you scribe the long edge first, you can run into problems. When you remove material from the short edge, the workpiece will shift down and ruin the nice fit you achieved on the back edge. By fitting the short-edge first, the distance that the piece shifts is less, any discrepancies in the fit are minimized because they occur on the shorter side.) Once the top fit snugly, it was glued and screwed from below.

The face frames for this project were built on-site using 2"-wide face frame stock that was already painted and ready to go. This allowed me to cut parts as I needed them and glue and nail them to the cabinet boxes. This was quicker and easier than building face frames as separate sub-assemblies in the shop. It also simplified the process of trimming out the tall bookcase by allowing me to position the pieces one at a time. I started with the long piece of trim on the right-hand side because it is the easy one. I aligned its edge with the outside of the bookcase, which I had already verified to be plumb. Once it was nailed on, I was ready to tackle the scribe strip on the left-hand side.

I knew I wanted the scribe strip to be 2" wide at the bottom so it was symmetrical with the right-hand side. Because I had a $3^{1}/_{2}$" wide scribe strip, I set my compass

STEP 21 ■ I rabbeted the back edge of a cap moulding to fit along the top edge of the beadboard.

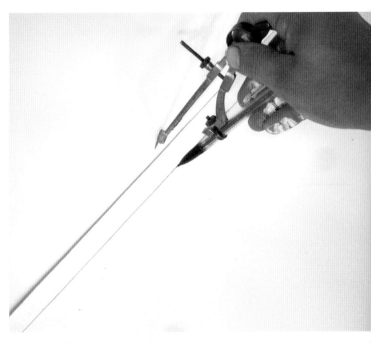

STEP 22 ■ To install the bench top, I sat it in place and used my compass to transfer the shape of the bookcase side and the back wall onto the bench top. I began with the bookcase because it is the shorter side.

STEP 23 ■ Once the top fit snugly against the side of the bookcase, I was ready to repeat the process on the back edge.

STEP 24 ■ I trimmed out the front of the bench with 2"-wide face-frame trim, which I attached with glue and brads. The nail holes were easy to touch up with some caulk and paint.

for $1^1/_2$" (the amount of material to be cut off the left-hand side of the strip). I positioned the scribe strip with its bottom edge against the wall and checked to make sure it was plumb. (Since I was working alone, I used a nail to hold it temporarily in place.) With both hands free, it was a simple matter to run the compass along the wall and establish a cut line. I pulled the scribe strip off, cut along the line and had a very nice fit. I glued and nailed it into place, then measured for the face frame trim at the top and bottom of the cabinet. With the face-frame trim completed, I installed the two pieces of crown moulding and the small moulding on the outside edge of the bookcase that covers the joint between the cabinet back and side.

STEP 25 ▪ Because it was the easiest piece to install, I attached the right-side face-frame trim on the bookcase first.

STEP 26 ■ The face-frame trim on the left-hand side didn't fit precisely against the wall, so it needed to be scribed. I used a level to set it plumb and tacked it temporarily into place.

STEP 27 ■ A compass transferred the wall's profile onto the edge of the face-frame trim. After jigsawing away the excess, it fit neatly. Installing the top and bottom pieces of face frame trim was easy.

STEP 28 ■ The crown moulding finished it off.

project four

formal library

THIS PROJECT WAS DESIGNED for an early 20th-century home with nice period details. My clients wanted a classic home library which would speak to the house's vintage but would still accommodate a few specific needs of their own. They didn't want a bunch of bookcases set against a wall. The goal was to completely reinvent the room with a new ambiance. It also needed to feature a home-office nook, space for a flat-screen TV and a place for a couch so that they could enjoy sitting and spending time in the room. We came up with a design that worked on all counts.

By using a dark, rich finish on cherry, we achieved a classic, old-world feel which provided a nice color contrast to the oak hardwood floors. The use of some architectural elements such as fluted columns and plinth blocks, frame-and-panel doors, and a large custom crown moulding all worked together to set a formal tone. My clients requested a lot of open shelving to display books and collectibles, with a few raised-panel doors below the window so that clutter can be easily hidden away. The antique brass hardware was a nice finishing touch.

The lighting plan was an essential part of the design. I planned for small puck lights to be set into each cabinet near the ceiling, which created lots of light and shadows while still providing adequate ambient light. The final effect is more rich and interesting than having a single ceiling fixture which would wash the whole room uniformly with light. The project required the services of a licensed electrician, who put in new outlets for the puck lights, moved a light switch and relocated two original wall sconces to a better spot.

This series of pictures shows how the library shaped up. The biggest design challenge was planning around the window, which wasn't centered on the wall. Ultimately, I decided to make components of different depths so that I could create a uniform reveal around the edges of the window and thereby create the illusion of symmetry.

design notes: responding to real-world job sites

Making this project successful required more than just building a set of boxes and putting them into place. The process of designing and building this library required coming up with a design concept and paying close attention to the setting so that the final result fit and worked perfectly. In other words, knowing what you want to build is only the first part of the process. Successfully adapting that idea to a real-world environment is just as important. This job site offered several challenges which required some problem-solving.

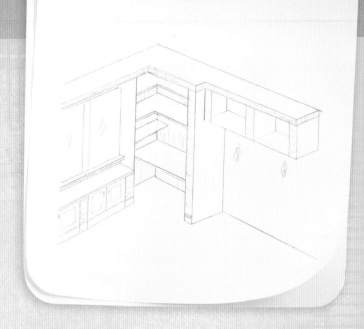

1. The window wasn't centered on the wall — I accommodated this by situating the home-office nook on the wider side (we needed the depth for the desktop) and by making the bookcase on the opposite side slightly deeper to create the illusion of symmetry.

2. We had hoped to place some bookshelves above the windows, but there just wasn't enough vertical space to fit them in. Rather than leaving the area empty, however, I felt it was critical to carry the woodwork across to establish the built-in feel that we were after. I decided to build a large valance above the windows. This allowed the crown moulding to run continuously around the room, and it also provided a place to install the puck lights, which were important not only for lighting but for design unity — each bay on each wall has a light in it. This rhythm needed to be consistent to achieve the formal, ordered effect that we wanted.

3. The ceilings were reasonably flat but they weren't perfectly level, so running the crown tight to the ceilings was tricky. I dealt with the variations by using a wider face-frame piece (a moulding rail) at the tops of the cabinets. This allowed me to adjust the placement of the crown moulding so it could hug the ceiling. The variations in the reveal on the rail is less noticeable than it would be on a narrower rail.

cabinet door layout & construction

The base cabinet on the north wall is long and not especially tall. This required some creativity when thinking through its design. I had originally designed the cabinet as a symmetrical, two-bay unit with two doors apiece. This looked fine on paper but when I started to build the cabinet, I quickly realized it would look awkward. As a rule of thumb, any cabinet door that is wider than it is tall should be divided into two doors. I did some head-scratching and divided the space into thirds, which was graceful.

All the doors are the same size, so the outside appearance is symmetrical and composed. The cabinet interiors are not the same size because of the wide vertical stiles, but this has no ramifications for anything else and is less important than the appearance of the entire unit.

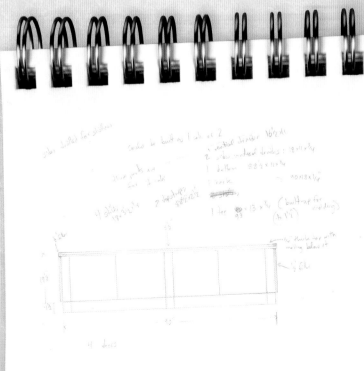

This type of project is different than the kitchen or bathroom projects where the components are rectangular boxes of similar size, which makes it easy to visualize how they'll all come together.

This project was challenging because it is composed of many different elements. The west wall features floor-to-ceiling bookcases, the north wall is dominated by a large window that I framed with a window seat and a light valance, the north-east corner contains an office nook with floor-to-ceiling wall paneling and the east wall has a couch and period light fixtures.

To guide me in my design and fabrication work, I decided to set up the various parts as I built them. This required a bit of space, but was well worth it. Even though I had a good plan which came from my drawings and site measurements, I was able to understand the intricacies of the design better when I was able to stand amidst the components and see how they fit together. I was also able to identify a couple of problem areas that weren't obvious on paper, and they were much easier to rectify early on in the shop than they would have been later on the job site.

Tip: **Leaving Room**

A large-scale project like this needs to be designed to allow for some wiggle room so you can make adjustments during the installation and accommodate various problems or inconsistencies in the job site. On the east wall, I planned for a gap between each bookcase that would be hidden behind the face-frame trim. The exact size of the gap didn't matter — I could position the bookcases as needed. This turned out to be of critical importance, because a light switch was located where it would have lined up on a bookcase side. Instead of having to move the light switch, I shuffled the cabinets a couple of inches.

STEP 1 ■ Mocking up the project in my shop helped me get a feel for the size of the project and how the various components would work together.

STEP 2 ■ This was critical to helping me design the transitions between the low bench and the tall bookcases. It also made the installation much easier because I had already walked through it in my shop.

STEP 3 ▪ The faux columns were built with long miters on their exposed corners. This gives them a seamless look.

STEP 4 ▪ Blue painters tape is the ultimate device for clamping an assembly like this.

STEP 5 ▪ The light valance (shown upside down) got a pair of "dog ears" on the ends — these pieces of wood allowed it to be simply set into place atop the faux columns.

STEP 6 ▪ The dog ears made it easy for one person to position the light valance.

STEP 8 ■ I attached the moulding to the edge of the desktop with glue and nails.

STEP 7 ■ The office nook went together quickly. I tacked it together in the shop because it would have to be disassembled and the parts would need to be trimmed to fit onsite.

STEP 9 ■ Cutting out the L-shaped shelves with a jigsaw took time but it produced a strong shelf, as compared to joining two rectangular sections.

L-shaped shelves

In order to make the most of the storage space in the office nook , I made some L-shaped shelves. The question was whether to cut them from one piece or to assemble them from two rectangles, which might be quicker and easier to cut out — which would give the best overall result? I opted to cut them from one piece because they would be stronger and wouldn't require any additional reinforcement. It seemed like it would make for a less efficient use of materials, but in the end I was able to use the strangely-shaped offcuts. The basic process was straightforward. I used a jigsaw to cut out the shelves, and then fine-tuned the cut edges with a random orbit sander. The front edges were then covered with iron-on veneer edge banding.

Tip: **On Bases**

For a long run of cabinets, cabinet bases can be composed of smaller bases that will be screwed together, or if you have the material and the inclination, one long base. There is no inherent advantage or disadvantage to either method — I like to use up scrap ³/₄" plywood on my bases, so the sizes of the scraps determine the sizes of the bases that I build. It is worth pointing out that there is no need to build bases that are identical in size if they're going to be combined into one long run. I recently had to build 11' (132") of cabinetry. I accomplished by building 3 bases of arbitrary sizes: 36", 44" and 52". When finished, they were covered with toe kick trim, so the lengths matter — as long as they added up to 132".

STEP 10 ▦ To level the cabinet bases, I set them in place and drew a level line on the wall above them at an arbitrary height.

STEP 11 ▦ I measured down from the line to the cabinet bases. This showed me where the floor was out of level. I shimmed up the low spots until the measurements were consistent.

If it wasn't already obvious, planning a project like this is time-consuming. Once the planning is under control, however, building the cabinets goes smoothly. As mentioned, with a project of this scale and complexity, I like to set it up full-scale in my shop as I build.

A critical part of the design, both practically and aesthetically, is the pair of faux columns on the north wall that flank the low base cabinet. They act as fillers which can be trimmed on-site if need be, and give visual heft to frame out the windows. I built them with long miters on the edges because they produce corners that are neat, clean and don't need to be trimmed or covered up. I have found that using masking tape on long miters works great

to hold them together. I lay the parts flat on the bench, pull them together tightly with the tape. Flip them over and glue up the joint.

The light valance is essentially two strips of veneered plywood that are screwed together at a 90° angle. The plywood edge on the bottom needs to be edge-banded, but the other edges will be hidden after the installation is complete. You can see that the light valance has an ear attached to each end so it can be set into position by one person. The ears will rest on top of the faux columns.

The desk nook is made up of panels that will be glued and screwed to the walls. They will be trimmed to exact size on site, but I tacked them in place in my shop so that

STEP 12 ▪ The bases were secured to the wall studs.

STEP 13 ▪ Before I could set the tall bookcases in place, I measure for a couple of electrical boxes. I transferred these measurements to the cabinet backs and made the corresponding cutouts.

STEP 14 ▪ I designed this run of cabinets to have a gap between each cabinet. The width of the gap wasn't important because it would be covered by face-frame trim, but it was necessary because it provided some wiggle room in setting the cabinets.

STEP 15 ▪ Once the vertical trim was in place, I cut the horizontal trim to size and attached it to the cabinets.

I could proceed with the construction process. The desktop has solid wood trim piece across its front edge and a hole with a grommet so cords and cables can be run through it. The desktop will need to be trimmed on site to fit into the nook. The L-shaped shelves are supported by cleats glued and nailed to the wall panels. Once the large upper cabinet is done, it can be hoisted into place and the construction phase is nearly complete.

INSTALLATION STEPS

Setting cabinet bases is more science than art, but there are a few nuances which help determine your approach. A small, simple installation will allow you to use a simple method while and a larger, more complex project will require a more sophisticated system.

Tip: **Extra Parts**

This project involves lots of long, straight trim pieces- crown moulding rails, face frame parts, and more. Experience has taught me that mistakes some times happen, and that some times situations arise that you just can't always anticipate- for example, maybe a wall that seemed plumb really isn't, so an additional filler strip might be necessary. In these cases, it is awfully convenient to have an extra part on hand. As I was milling the trim for this project, I ripped an extra piece of stock to the widest dimension that I was likely to need (96" × 4"), and added it in with all of the other parts that I was sanding and finishing. I didn't even notice the small amount of additional time that it required, and I sure was glad when I actually did end up using it. Having it ready to use saved a lot of time and hassle in not having to run back to the shop and repeat the entire finishing sequence again (waiting for all those coats to dry, etc.)

STEP 16 ■ The faux columns pressed neatly into place between the tall bookcase and the low bench.

STEP 17 ■ I trimmed this transition area with a piece of face-frame trim.

THE SIMPLE BASE METHOD

Set a level on a cabinet base and just shim it as necessary until it is level. This is quick, easy and it works if:

1. The cabinet or run of cabinets is not longer than your longest level .

2. The cabinet(s) don't need to be an exact height.

3. The cabinet(s) don't turn a corner and continue down an adjacent wall.

THE COMPLEX BASE METHOD

You will begin the project by drawing a level line around the room on all the walls that will have cabinet bases set on them. For this project, that means the west and north walls. A level line can be established with a laser level, but for those who don't have one, here's what I do.

Using a long level, I start by drawing a line at an arbitrary height. The only criteria is that it be at a convenient

STEP 18 ■ To create the office nook, I cut a piece of $^1/4$" cherry plywood to size and secured it to the wall.

STEP 19 ■ The other faux column covered up the edge of the plywood and boxed-in the other side of the window.

STEP 20 ■ The faux column was screwed to the bench through its side.

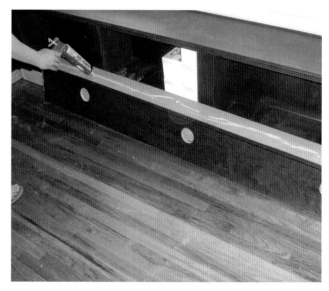

STEP 21 ■ The light valance was secured to the wall with construction adhesive and brad nails.

working height relative to the bases — about 12" above the bases is fine. I extend the line, keeping the level's bubble precisely centered. Wrapping around a corner is easy. Set the level at the height of the mark on the first wall, then raise or lower the other end of the level to create a

level line. Extend this line as far as necessary. Having a second pair of hands makes this process easier.

Once I have a level line, I measure from it down to the bases at approximately 15" intervals. I record the measurements on the wall and then step back to assess the

STEP 22 ▪ The other side of the office nook was constructed of ³/₄" plywood. I had to scribe the back edge to fit it against the slightly irregular plaster wall.

STEP 23 ▪ The desktop dropped into place and was supported by cleats on three sides.

Tip: **Fluted Columns**

The fluted columns are a pretty big element in the design, and the way they terminate at the floor is important. I decided to build three-dimensional bump outs beneath each one to create the impression that the columns and the face frame trim behind them continued all the way to the floor. I need to do this, however, in a way that allowed for adjustment on the job site, since there was a possibility that the bases would need to be shimmed up, and I couldn't make assumptions about how high these bump out would need to be. My solution was to make them in the shop beforehand, and to make them about 1" higher than the toe kicks themselves (5¹/₂" tall). I knew that I wouldn't need the full 1" of wiggle room, but it didn't hurt to have it. And then, once the bases were shimmed to level and the face frames were installed in their final locations, it was easy to measure for the heights of the bump outs and install them with construction adhesive. I then ran the toe kick trim between the bump outs using simple butt joints—no need for mitered corners.

Tip: **Edge-Banding**

A couple of years ago, I finally bought a dedicated edge-banding machine. It is one of the most important tools that I own, but it is an expensive machine that requires frequent use to justify its high cost. Before I had it, I applied miles and miles of edge banding with an iron. For years this was my only option, but then I moved to a larger city and discovered that I was able to outsource the edge banding on bigger projects. By calling around, I located a couple of cabinet shops that didn't mind running my panels through their own machines. I found that if you have a large number of panels and your time is tight, it might be worth it. If you've only got a handful of panels, it probably wouldn't be worth the time and effort of loading them up, dropping them off and picking them up.

STEP 24 ■ The vertical trim on the right-hand side of the office nook helped to give it a substantial and finished look.

STEP 25 ■ The L-shaped shelves fit neatly into place and were also supported by cleats.

STEP 26 ■ It took two people to hoist the upper cabinet into place and get it secured to the wall. The design dictated that it be set down a few inches from the ceiling to provide room for the lights.

STEP 27 ■ I had a unique crown moulding milled for this project. It made a great transition between the cabinets and the ceiling.

numbers. The goal here is to identify the highest spot on the floor. If you're lucky, the numbers are all the same and you can screw the bases to studs and move on. In reality, the numbers often vary. This method allows you to see exactly where and how much the floors vary from flat and level. The smallest number corresponds with the highest point on the floor. The bases must be shimmed up until measurements taken at those other spots are equal to the measurement taken at the high spot. You'll also need to use a level to check from front-to-back on the bases and shim under the front edges of the bases as needed.

UP FROM THE BASE

Setting the bases can be time-consuming, but once it is done, things move quickly. In this case, the three wall cab-

inets on the west wall could go in as soon as I measured the light switch and outlets on the wall, transferred these measurements to the backsides of the cabinets and made the appropriate cutouts. Once the cabinets had been set in place, I screwed them to studs in the back wall. I covered the screw holes with self-adhesive cherry screw covers and then stained them.

The face-frame trim pieces were attached with construction adhesive and nails, as were the crown moulding rails. The vertical pieces didn't need to be cut to any particular length because they would be hidden by the crown moulding.

With the major components set into place on the west wall, I turned my attention to the north wall. I measured and marked the wall so that I could see where the faux

STEP 28 ■ The toe-kick trim needed to be scribed.

STEP 29 ■ Once the doors were hung, the bench took on a regal appearance.

STEP 30 ■ I used fluted half-columns to embellish all of the vertical face-frame trim.

column would go, and then I screwed a 2×4 to the wall to serve as a nailer for the faux column. I screwed one of the faux columns onto the left side of the base cabinet and set this subassembly on the cabinet bases. I wiggled it into position, secured the cabinet to the wall and the faux column to the nailer. I attached the bench top using screws from below. With the faux column in place, I was able to attach the final piece of face-frame trim on the east wall. This made a smooth transition between the woodwork on the two walls.

The wall paneling on the east wall of the office nook was held in place with construction adhesive and nails. The exact fit of the first panel wasn't critical because all four edges would be covered. I sized it about $1/2$" too small all around so it would fit easily, even with variations in the flatness and squareness of the walls and floor.

I framed in the right side of the window by attaching the other faux column to the right side of the base cabinet, and then I installed the light valance like I did in the shop during the mock up. This time I used construction adhesive on the back side where it met the wall. You'll notice that this method of framing-in the window makes the site work go fairly easily. I didn't have to cut down any of the components or add any fillers. I had planned from the beginning for a small consistent reveal around the existing window casing, which not only looked nice but it meant that I didn't have to fit my components with super-human precision. I just needed to center the base cabinet and light valance on the window, and that would automatically make the left- and right-hand side reveals

architectural elements

BEYOND THE BASIC BOX

It is easy to fall into the trap of building a bunch of boxes and setting them next to each other and calling it a day. Although this approach is well suited to a lot of the modern, minimalist designs that I create for my clients, it falls short when you are trying to create a more elaborate look.

You can add some character and variety to your designs by incorporating pre-fabricated or shop-made architectural elements. In this case, I relied on fluted half-columns as a major visual element of the design. They are positioned between the various units at regular intervals and contribute to the formal, ordered feel that we wanted.

My client also wanted a unique crown moulding for the library, so I had a 6" crown milled from solid cherry by a local millwork shop. It's simple — just a big cove without a lot of frills — and it mirrors a period detail found in other rooms of the home.

This example is just the tip of the iceberg. I recommend visiting Van Dyke's Restorer's Hardware online. You'll find the following:

- brackets & corbels for shelves, mantles, etc.
- lots of crown mouldings (including built-up and multiple-part profiles)
- chair rails
- wainscoting
- wood paneling — for example, flat panels with mitered sticking
- turned cabinet legs (also for corners) and other bun feet in various shapes & sizes

consistent. If I had planned to set the columns up against the window casing, not only would it have looked too crowded, but it would have made more scribing and trimming work necessary.

With the major components in place on the north wall, I concentrated on the east wall. I set the ³/₄" wall panel into place and screwed it to studs. I used a level before attaching it to make sure that the right-hand edge was plumb. If it hadn't been, I would have had to trim it accordingly. Then I set up the office nook partition and screwed it to edge of the ³/₄" panel. I already had cleats in place for the desktop, so that dropped right in. After nailing on the face-frame trim to the right side of the nook, I turned my attention to the L-shaped shelves, which I installed on cleats that I put up on site.

The large upper cabinet took two people to hoist into place. Once it was in, I wired up the lights and attached the face-frame trim. At this point, all of the big stuff was done. All I had to do was put up the crown moulding, hang the doors on the base cabinet, attach the fluted trim on the face frame stiles and attach the toe kick trim, scribing where necessary. As a final touch, I built small bump outs below the face frame stiles and attached the plinth blocks.

STEP 31 ■ I used some special plinth blocks to trim the cabinet bases below the half-columns — they provided a nice traditional look.

door construction

The six flat-panel cabinet doors are all identical, which makes for an efficient construction process. I cut the grooves and the tenons on the table saw using a dado blade. When I have a set of identical doors like this, I don't always take the time to dry-fit every door. I figure that if one goes together, then the others should too, since the parts are identical and were made at the same time using the same process. I also save time and hassle by clamping a few doors in each set of clamps, which also requires fewer clamps.

The moulding that I chose for the door panels provides a nice period detail. The profile wasn't critical in this case. I wanted something that would be period-appropriate and complement the design.

For safety's sake, I recommend routing the profile on the edge of a larger piece of stock and then ripping off the part you'll use for the moulding. These $3/4" \times 1/2"$ pieces of moulding would have been too small for me to safely and smoothly feed past my router bit, so I began with $1\,1/4" \times 3/4"$ blanks.

The mouldings were so small that I had a hard time cutting them with my power miter saw, so I used a miter box and a hand saw to get clean cuts. I don't think this ended up taking much longer. I used cyanoacrylate adhesive (superglue) with a fast-acting catalyst to glue the mouldings in place.

STEP 1 ■ Using a dado stack in my table saw, I grooved the rails and stiles of all the doors to accept the panels.

STEP 2 ■ Using the same dado stack, I set my saw with a stand-off block attached to the fence for a safer cut. I then ran the tenons (using multiple cuts) on the rails.

STEP 3 ■ Even though I wanted a flat-panel look for the doors, I also wanted a $1/2"$-thick solid panel, so I raised the back face of the panels on my router table using a panel-raising bit.

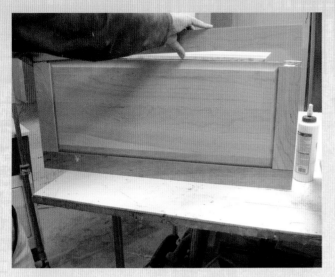

STEP 4 ■ Door assembly is standard, but pay attention and keep the best face forward.

STEP 5 ■ A good set of well-used pipe clamps makes quick work of gluing up the doors by ganging three at a time.

STEP 6 ■ The moulding is made on the router table, but don't try to run a piece this small. Start with a larger board, run the moulding profile, then cut the moulding away from the board to the finished size. Make a jointer pass on the cut edge of the blank and start the process over. A little time consuming, but safe.

STEP 7 ■ After mitering and final fitting, the mouldings are ready to install on the doors.

project five

entertainment center

MY CLIENTS WERE RENOVATING the living room of their 1970's home in favor of a more modern look and they recognized a great opportunity in the outdated and under utilized area around the fireplace. I worked directly with a local artisan who specializes in interior concrete work, and together we came up with a plan to build a concrete mantle and a bamboo entertainment center that would become a focal point for the new design.

Our concept required the concrete mantle to span the wall above the firebox and extend all the way to the wall on the right-hand side of the room. The entertainment center had to be planned and built accordingly. The installation was complicated and it required us to think carefully about the sequence of the required steps. In short, we had the do things right, but we also had to do them in the right order.

Building the cabinets was straightforward. They were typical of the frameless (European-style) cabinetry that I build a lot. The bases were made of ³/₄"-thick melamine scraps. I build a lot of cabinets that get covered by concrete countertops, and, in such cases, I reinforce the cabinets. For example, I build bases that are beefier, and I use ³/₄"-thick cabinet backs. In this situation, however, the cabinets weren't really bearing any of the weight of the mantle, so I built the cabinets accordingly. I mention this because I think it's important to consider the final application of the cabinets as they're being designed and crafted.

This project made use of ³/₄" bamboo plywood, which I had been purchasing online for the past few years, but my regular suppliers recently began to carry it as an in-stock item. The sustainable attributes of the material are getting a lot of media attention and that was an important factor for my client. They also appreciated its unique look, which suited our contemporary project perfectly. I faced a small dilemma, however, when it came to edge-banding the cabinet boxes. I was able to find bamboo edge-banding easily enough, but it did not come pre-glued. I solved this problem by using Fastedge double-sided contact adhesive. Once I got the hang of it, it was quick and easy to use, and it was superior to using spray adhesive, which is messy no matter how careful you are. I used ³/₄" melamine for the cabinet construction for all the usual reasons — economy, ease and the time it saves by being pre-finished. In addition, its relative economy helped to offset the extremely high cost of the bamboo.

This was the state of this area when my client purchased the house. It offered us an opportunity to create a useful and attractive built-in that became the focal point for the entire room.

STEP 1 ■ I couldn't find any bamboo edge banding that came pre-glued, so I used double-sided edge tape, which worked like a charm once I got the hang of it.

designing for a simpler installation

I have learned that it pays to plan ahead to keep snags to a minimum on job sites. In this case, I made an observation early on that turned out to be critical. I had the option of bringing the cabinetry flush with the front of the wall where the fireplace is located, but I used a long straightedge to check out the straightness of that surface, and sure enough, it was not completely flat. If I had built cabinets in anticipation of bringing them flush with this crooked edge, I would've opened up a can of worms — the discrepancy of a flat cabinet against a crooked edge would need to be dealt with using some type of trim moulding, and that would have meant extra trips back and forth, and I also would have lost the clean look that I wanted. So, my solution was to shorten the depth of the cabinets so that they sat back about two inches from the edges. The discrepancy was then minimized to the point where it wasn't noticeable — and I saved myself from an unanticipated problem. Sometimes it is easiest to solve job-site challenges by avoiding them in the first place.

working within a captured space

This project is challenging to install because the cabinets are surrounded on both sides by walls. A very common method for fitting components into spaces like this involves the use of filler strips. The basic concept requires you to build the components slightly smaller than the size of the opening and then fill in the gaps on the sides with pieces of trim called filler strips. The filler strips can be trimmed to fit around any irregularities in the surface of the drywall. Filler strips are also frequently used at the end of a run of cabinets to close a gap and create a true built-in look. This chapter shows how to use a compass to scribe filler strips to fit, and the included DVD will demonstrate this process in greater detail.

STEP 2 ▪ Mocking-up a project in the shop is critical for me. It helps me identify any potential problems that might arise, and, it is good practice for the installation itself.

STEP 3 ▪ This project is complex in that it features an integrated concrete mantle. By elevating the upper cabinets on a pair of separate bases, I created a space for the mantle to run. The bases could be trimmed or shimmed as needed to fit the mantle.

This entertainment center was unusual in that it featured an integrated concrete mantle that spanned the entire wall. I knew that this unique design element would be beautiful, but it introduced a few complexities that had to be addressed right away. For one thing, I needed to work directly with the concrete fabricator to determine the exact size and position of the mantle, because it would in turn determine the size of the cabinets. We also had to decide on an approach that would provide the best result with a minimum amount of hassle during the installation. I try to plan for some adjustability in all of my installations — hence the use of filler strips, shims and the like — but this was complicated by the fact that the mantle weighed over 300 pounds and couldn't be jostled once it was set into place. This meant that the adjustment I knew I would need had to be achieved via the cabinets themselves. I decided to build bases that could be shimmed as necessary. This applied to both the upper and lower units, as illustrated in the photos.

In this project, the order of operations was critical to having the various components fit precisely, and mocking up the installation in the shop helped me to understand

STEP 4 ■ The right-hand upper cabinet needed to be built from bamboo rather then melamine because it wouldn't be covered by any doors.

STEP 5 ■ During the installation, I worked directly with the concrete fabricator to determine the spot where he planned to position the mantle. This determined the point to which I would shim my cabinet bases.

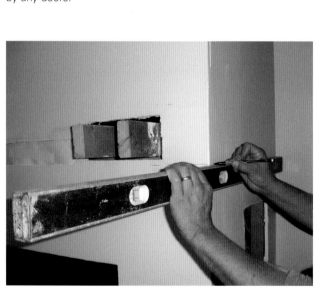

STEP 6 ■ Once I had established the height of the bottom of the mantle, I used a level and drew a line.

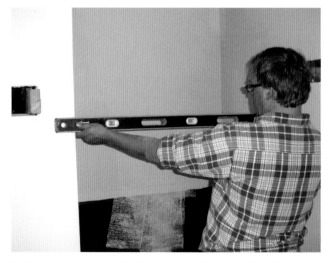

STEP 7 ■ I extended this line across all three walls of the nook where the cabinets would be placed.

exactly how the sequence would work. I knew that I would set base cabinets first, and that I would raise them, using shims and scrap plywood, to the height of the bottom of the mantle. The mantle would then be set into place and I would put in the base for the upper cabinets. If necessary, it could be shimmed up to create a level platform for the upper cabinets. I could then set the upper cabinets, secure them to the walls and to each other.

INSTALLATION STEPS

I scheduled the installation to ensure that the concrete fabricator and I were there at the same time. This turned out to be very helpful. My first and most important question for him was how high the bottom of the mantle was, and once he marked this critical spot on the wall, I was good to go. I used a level to transfer this measurement across the walls of the niche where the cabinets would go, and began to level the bases. I did this by taking the total measurement from the line to the floor and recording the numbers on the wall at each corner of the base. The numbers varied $1/4$", which put an exact number on the slope of the floor. I was then able to subtract the height of the cabinets from the numbers and that told me how high the base needed to be in each of its respective corners. I shimmed accordingly and came up with a configuration that was level and would also put the top of my cabinet at the right height to align with the mantle. I screwed the base to the back wall and was ready to move on.

Before setting the cabinets in place, I had to cut out around a couple of outlets. One outlet was controlled by

STEP 8 ■ By measuring down from the line and subtracting the height of the cabinets, I could see how high the bases needed to be.

STEP 9 ■ I set the bases into place and shimmed accordingly.

STEP 10 ■ Because these cabinets were going to hold audio-visual equipment, I needed to integrate an outlet. We had a licensed electrician install another outlet with a separate wall switch to control the lights that I would be installing later.

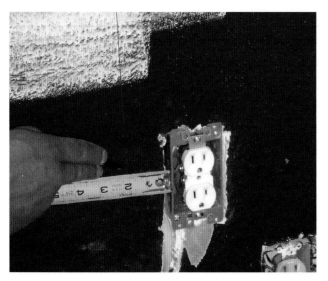

STEP 11 ▪ To figure out exactly where the outlet fell, I drew a vertical line where the edge of the cabinet would go and measured from it to the outlet.

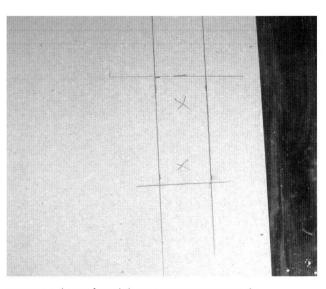

STEP 12 ▪ I transferred these measurements to the cabinet back

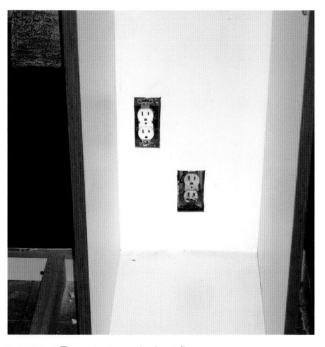

STEP 13 ▪ The cutouts worked out fine.

STEP 14 ▪ Once I measured the depth of the mantle and the depth of the nook, I realized that the cabinets would have to be bumped out 1" from the back wall. I hadn't planned on this, but it was an easy fix. I screwed two layers of scrap $1/2$" plywood to the studs.

ventilation for audio visual components

Some stereo and video components can generate a lot of heat. One obvious way of dealing with this is to place the components in an open cabinet, but in this case, we wanted to tuck them away behind a solid door. To play it safe, we installed a small fan in the cabinet and cut some holes that allowed the hot air to be expelled through the open bookcase in the upper half of the unit. We also placed the equipment on slotted shelves. Serious audiophiles can be more fussy about the shelf materials and construction methods, so this is worth researching online if you're interested.

cable routing/cord management

To make it easier to run cables between the components in the cabinet, I cut scalloped notches at the back of each shelf. You can find more convenient (and more expensive) pullouts that allow you to slide the components out for easy access if you look around. I recommend Accuride as a good supplier. The cable that ran from the TV to the cabinet had to be in place prior to installing the entertainment center. All we needed to do was cut a hole in the side of the cabinet in the appropriate spot so that the cable could be connected.

STEP 15 ■ Before screwing the cabinet to the rear wall, I double-checked its alignment with a level.

STEP 16 ■ With the base cabinets in place, the concrete fabricator test-fit the mantle and then prepped the area for its installation. It took four of us to lift it into place, but it went quite smoothly.

a wall switch and it would be used to power the halogen lights that I would be installing later, and the other outlet would be dedicated to the stereo components. To make the cutouts, I first had to know where the cabinet would be positioned. I measured from the wall and drew a plumb line to indicate the edge of the cabinet. I then measured from this line to the edges of the outlet and transferred these measurements to the cabinet back. After double-checking my measurements, it was a simple matter to connect the dots and draw in the cut lines.

A minor glitch emerged when we realized that the cabinets would need to be furred-out from the back wall. The mantle wasn't as deep as I had planned, and the only way to make up this distance was by bringing the cabinets out an inch. This was handled by fastening a couple of layers of ¹/₂" scrap plywood to the studs. With this blocking in place, I had no problem securing the cabinets to the

STEP 17 ■ With the upper cabinet bases in place, the upper cabinet could be installed. You'll notice they overlap the mantle to create a very clean transition between the two elements.

STEP 18 ■ Hanging the cabinet doors gave us a taste for how the finished product would look.

STEP 19 ■ A little bit of drywall repair was necessary where the mantle slid into the wall, but it didn't hold up the cabinet installation.

STEP 20 ■ I had to install a filler strip on the sides of the cabinets next to the walls.

STEP 21 ■ With the filler strips in place, the project took on a truly built-in feel.

remote access

Most remote controls are useless if the audio/visual components are stashed behind a solid door. To get around this, my client used an inexpensive remote control extender which transmits the remote's signal perfectly from anywhere in the room. I recommend Crutchfield (crutchfield.com) as a good source for reliable equipment and information.

STEP 23 ■ Before installing the toe-kick trim, I cut the shims back with a sharp utility knife.

STEP 22 ■ The fillers were slightly wider on the right-hand side than the left because the cabinets were not exactly centered in the opening. This is because one of the outlets on the back wall would have fallen directly behind the cabinet side. So, I set the cabinets a couple of inches to the left. The end result looked great and this minor issue wasn't a problem.

wall. I made sure to double-check the alignment of the units with a level as I progressed. The right-hand cabinet went in easily, and the concrete fabricator got the mantle moved in and the area prepped for its installation.

Once I set the upper base into place and checked it for level, the upper cabinets were set into position. They overlapped neatly onto the concrete to create a nice, clean transition. The wall required a bit of patching around the mantle but that was unavoidable.

Once the cabinets were secured to the wall and to each other, I proceeded with the final details of the installation. I had to put in four filler strips to create transitions with the walls and establish a true built-in look. I got lucky here. These were some of the flattest walls I had ever seen and three out of four strips didn't even need to be scribed to fit. I measured the gaps at their top and bottoms and ripped strips to press into place. This worked out great. I screwed through the strips using long screws so that I could hit the studs in the walls on the other side. This provided a tight fit and a secure connection.

STEP 24 ■ I measured the height at both ends of the opening for the toe-kick trim. As luck would have it, the measurements were the same.

STEP 25 ■ Construction adhesive and brad nails secured the toe kick trim.

STEP 26 ■ I needed to drill a couple of holes between the cabinet boxes so my clients could plug in all of their AV gear.

STEP 27 ■ To install the lights and run the wire, I started by drilling a small hole near the back edge of the cabinet bottom.

installing in-cabinet lighting

Lighting was key to this design. I installed four puck lights on the shelves in the upper bookcase. This achieved a few things: It created drama by creating areas of light and shadow, it helped draw the eye upward and emphasize the high ceilings —a dramatic feature in and of themselves. Installing the lights is simply a matter of installing a few screws. I made sure to build this cabinet a few inches shallower than the others so there was space behind it to run the cord.

STEP 28 ▪ I also needed to notch the back edges of the floating shelves to run the wiring.

Before applying the toe-kick trim, I cut off the shims which were protruding below the cabinet. A utility knife works great to score the shims, which will then break off evenly at that spot. I created a tightly-fitting piece of toe-kick trim by measuring the opening from top-to-bottom on both ends (the measurements varied by $1/8$") and then tapering my trim piece correspondingly. I dry-fit it to make sure it would work, and then applied construction adhesive when I was ready.

With all of the actual woodworking completed, I turned my attention to some of the functional aspects of the projects. To enable my client to run cords between the

STEP 29 ▪ I ran the wires to the light on the top sides of the shelves so they weren't visible.

cabinets, I drilled some $1^1/2$"-diameter holes where they were needed and I drilled a couple of $3/4$"-diameter holes so I could run the wires for the halogen lights up into the bookcase. I notched the back edges of the shelves for the wiring to run through and drilled a hole in the center of the shelves so I could place the wires on the top side of the shelves where they wouldn't be noticeable.

project six

kitchen

KITCHENS ARE OFTEN CONSIDERED the quintessential built-ins, and they have the potential to be complicated. Like all built-ins, they need to be both beautiful and functional. Satisfying both of those goals requires careful attention to the space that you have to work with and the practical needs of the people who are going to be using the space day in and day out.

This chapter doesn't pretend to be an exhaustive guide to kitchen planning — that is a topic that deserves a book of its own — but it will detail how I installed the cabinetry and related components that I built for a recent project.

This new kitchen was part of a large and time-consuming project. The lower photo shows a section of the center wall that was to be removed, but doing this came with high price tag, so the center island was converted into a peninsula. The photo at right shows the intersection of different ceiling heights. I designed cabinets that ended just below the lowest point.

BASE CABINET CONSTRUCTION

Once I have the kitchen planned out, I begin the shop work by building the cabinet bases. I like to do this because I always lay out the bases in my shop in the same configuration they will take in the finished kitchen. This helps me to visualize the project as it's coming together and also foresee any potential problems. It keeps finished cabinets from sitting directly on the floor and getting their edges dinged up, a condition I have heard called "shop

rash". Most cabinet bases are simple rectangles, but occasionally they are more interesting, as on a corner cabinet.

In this case, I built the cabinets out of white melamine. It is standard in most kitchens for a number of reasons. It is economical, durable, easily cleanable and it saves time because you don't have to apply a finish to it. The base cabinets went together with butt joints. I used brad nails to tack them together and then reinforced the joints with countersunk screws. I use nails the nails because they

STEP 1 ■ I always build cabinet bases first so I have a safe place to set the finished cabinets. This keeps the bottom edges of the cabinet from getting damaged.

STEP 2 ■ Most cabinet bases are simple rectangles, but corner bases are more complicated.

STEP 3 ■ The cabinets were constructed from 3/4" melamine panels that were assembled into a U-shape.

STEP 4 ■ The backs were glued and screwed after being tacked into place with brad nails.

STEP 5 ■ The backs for the upper cabinets were set into grooves milled into the panels. This is important because the cabinets will be attached to the wall through their backs, so the backs need to be tightly secured to the cabinets.

STEP 6 ■ The cabinets were assembled with countersunk screws.

STEP 7 ■ For complex projects, I always mock up the installation in the shop.

allow me to assemble the cabinets without using clamps, which saves a lot of time and effort.

The upper cabinets were built differently. Instead of nailing on the backs, I used a dado blade to cut a groove on the inside of the cabinet parts, with the backs fitting inside the groove. This is a nice way to ensure that the back is on securely because these cabinets will be fastened to a wall through the back. When I build cabinet boxes out of melamine, I use Roo Glue, which is the only adhesive I've found that sticks to this otherwise hard-to-bond-to surface. I have a set of inexpensive corner clamps that work handily for assembling parts such as these.

While most of the cabinets in this project weren't complicated, their eventual layout did require some thoughtful work in the shop. The peninsula, for example, posed a couple of contradictory challenges. I wanted to build it in as simple of a way as possible, so that the installation would go smoothly, but if I built it as one big unit, it would be too big to pick up and deliver. I decided to construct it in two long sections which I placed back to back. This worked out great. The sections were small enough to be maneuverable with the help of an assistant, and they went together easily on-site. I capped off the end with a finished panel that matched the cabinet doors. Mocking the assembly up in my shop helped me to problem-solve and ensure that this approach would work as I had hoped.

INSTALLATION

I began the installation with a general site inspection. This means taking a minute to look around and see what stands out. I look for surfaces that are visibly out of level or plumb, cutouts that will need to be made for electrical, plumbing, or HVAC components and any areas where there is pre-existing trim to be removed or taken into consideration. Once I got an overall feel for the job site, I started bringing things in.

STEP 8 ■ To level the cabinet bases, I drew a level line across all of the walls where the cabinets will run. I used a long level for this. Having an assistant helped. I measured down to the top of the cabinet bases from this line and shimmed up accordingly until all of the measurements were equal.

STEP 9 ■ I rechecked everything with a level once the shims were in place.

Tip: **Pre-hung Doors**

Having the doors pre-hung (although not precisely adjusted) in the shop will save time on-site. It also serves to verify that the doors will actually fit! I only say this because I once failed to do this and I realized on site that a door didn't fit and needed to be trimmed down—easy work with a jointer and stationary belt sander—but I didn't have the right tools on-site so I had to take a trip back to the shop. As a corollary, if you spend too much time getting the fits perfect in the shop, you'll probably have to re-adjust them once the cabinets are actually set into place. Another lesson learned the hard way. Another job-site time saver is having the door pulls attached prior to installation. This may not save any time, per se, but it shifts the time to the shop where you are free to make a mess, and away from the job site, which I like to keep as neat as

possible. Working in the shop is also, for me, much less stressful in general, so any time that I can do work there, I prefer to do so.

STEP 10 ■ Once the bases were level and secure, the cabinet boxes were set in place. They needed to be screwed together so their front edges were flush.

STEP 11 ■ I then screwed the cabinets to the rear wall.

Using my original drawings as a guideline, I set the cabinet bases into their approximate positions so I could get a sense of how the components would all fit together. In these situations, I always start in the corner and work outward because corners don't give you any wiggle room for adjustment. I had designed in enough space to use filler strips on the far ends of the cabinet runs if needed, so the logical progression was to start on the end that you can't adjust and work towards the part that you can.

With the bases in their approximate positions, I screwed them together so they functioned as one long base. My goal wasn't to install one cabinet perfectly, it was to install an entire run of cabinets as a unit that fit perfectly. This mindset is important, because it helps me to not focus too much on individual aspects of the job at the expense of proceeding well with the job as a whole.

At this point, I drew a level line on the wall and measured down from it to locate the high and low spots in the floor. Using a level and shims, I gradually built up the bases so that they were completely level. Once the bases were level, I secured them by screwing them into studs. The bases were then ready for cabinets. I brought in the cabinets (its nice to have some help for this) and placed them on the bases in their final locations. Again, I started with the corner and worked out from there. My time and effort in leveling the bases paid off, because the cabinets sat nice and level without any further shimming required.

I began securing the cabinets by clamping their front edges together. This is more important at this point than screwing them tightly to the wall because the best end-result requires the front edges to be flush so the doors hang in the same plane. And be advised — walls in new construction can have plenty of dips and low spots. Once the entire run of cabinets has been screwed together and you have a nice neat front edge, you can begin to screw the cabinets to the studs in the back wall. But be careful, keeping the front edges of the cabinets in a straight line is critical, so, I check it constantly with a straight edge. If there are dips or swells in the wall, the cabinets may need to be shimmed out on the low spots to preserve the straight front edge.

In a kitchen installation, it is inevitable that you'll need to make cutouts in the backs and/or bottoms of cabinets to accommodate electrical outlets or plumbing fixtures. To pin down the exact locations of these cutouts, I draw a vertical line on the wall to indicate where the side of

STEP 12 ▪ To identify the exact locations of the plumbing and electrical cutouts, I drew a vertical line representing the edge of the cabinet side. I then measured from it to the fixtures and transferred these measurements to the cabinet back.

STEP 13 ▪ After double-checking my measurements, I made the necessary cutouts and the cabinet fit great.

STEP 14 ◾ I also made a cutout so a gas line could be run to a wall oven.

STEP 15 ◾ Once the base cabinets were secured, I put up the wall cabinets. Cabinet jacks are invaluable for this.

the cabinet will fall, and then I measure over from that to whatever I need to cut around. I also measure up from the top of the cabinet base. I then transfer these numbers to the back of the cabinet so I can make the cutouts accurately. This is an example of the need to measure twice and cut once. I also suggest making sure that you are transferring the measurements correctly, i.e., measuring from the correct edge of the cabinet when you mark for the cutouts. I will admit that I once made a series of perfect cutouts that were all laid out from the left side of the cabinet when it should've been the right. Making a new cabinet back was my only choice at that point.

In this project, I also had to make a large notch in a cabinet back and bottom to accommodate an electrical outlet for a wall oven and a gas line.

Because of the unusual dimensions of the wall ovens, I needed to build a base to set inside the cabinet that housed them. It, too, would need to be notched around the electrical outlet and gas line in the back. By consulting the manufacturer's instructions and examining the ovens in person, I was able to ascertain how much space to allow for them to fit in. I trimmed the front opening of the cabinet accordingly and the ovens both fit perfectly.

Once the base cabinets were in, I grabbed my cabinet jacks to get ready to hang the upper cabinets. I marked the wall at the place where the bottom edge of the cabinet will need to be. This measurement has been determined in the planning stages, and it is in the range of 16-20" above the top of the finished counter. In this case, we were using 18". I needed to add on 2" for the thickness of the countertops that weren't yet in place, so I measured up 20" and set my cabinet jacks to that height. I used a level to draw a plumb line up from the edge of the base cabinet which helped me align the upper cabinet with it. As with the base cabinets, I began the upper cabinet installation in the corner and worked my way out.

A word to the wise: If you have more than a couple of cabinets to install, it is worth buying or making a set of cabinet jacks. They make an otherwise draining task easy and enjoyable. I used to use milk crates and shims of scrap wood — that works okay in a pinch.

In this project, the refrigerator was covered on one side by a finished cherry panel, which helps to create a professional, built-in look. The refrigerator panel butts up to a base cabinet, which creates a nice, simple transition between them. The upper cabinet also butts up to the refrigerator panel — with no need for a filler. In addition to looking good, this helps support the upper cabinet on the left side. The refrigerator panel should be installed after the base and upper cabinets are in place. This makes it easy the install it. Just set the panel in place and screw it to the cabinet sides. Metal L-brackets on the opposite side of the panel can be screwed into the back wall for additional support. Then the upper cabinet above the refrigerator can be installed — with a filler on the left-side if needed. In this case the fit was right on with no need for a filler. Sometimes you get lucky!

When installing drawer fronts, I start with the bottom one and work my way up, using shims to create a uniform gap between the drawer fronts. I use double-stick tape to hold the drawer fronts in place long enough to get a clamp on and drive some screws from inside the drawers.

Assembling the peninsula was straightforward — just as I had planned. Since it was built in two long strips

Tip: **Space Above**

During the design phase for this project, I realized that I needed to be careful in determining the height of the upper cabs. I noticed that the ceiling wasn't perfectly flat where it intersected the back wall, and so I decided not to take the cabinets all the way up. In fact, I sized them so that they would come down a full 2" from the ceiling, so that any disparities would be less noticeable, and this worked out nicely.

STEP 17 ■ Turning the adjustment screws on the hinges will move the doors in all planes — up and down, side-to-side and front-to-back.

STEP 16 ■ I attached the 3/4"-thick refrigerator panel to the base cabinet. This gave me a place to anchor the side of the corresponding upper cabinet as well.

STEP 18 ■ The wall ovens fit snugly into a base cabinet and one of them needed to sit on a raised platform inside the cabinet. Fortunately, I had the manufacturer's specs beforehand so I was ready.

STEP 19 ■ I like to hang my drawer fronts on site. I start at the bottom of each cabinet and use shims to create a uniform gap.

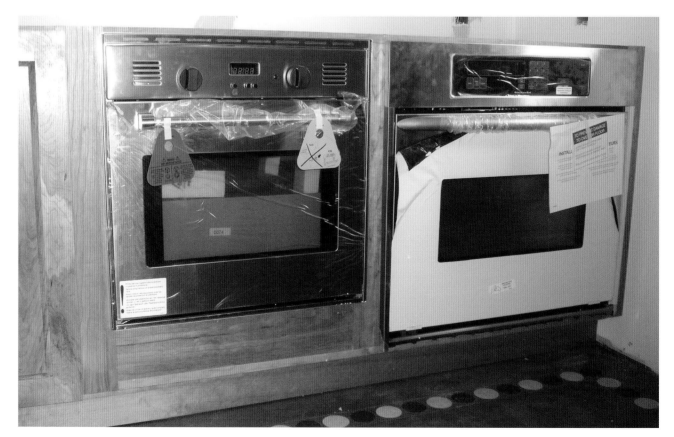

STEP 20 ■ I trimmed out the front of the oven cabinets as needed, and the result was a perfect built-in look.

STEP 21 ▪ The peninsula was built in two, long sections that backed up against each other. I screwed them together on site and capped the exposed end with a solid-wood panel.

STEP 22 ▪ The floors were slightly out of level, so I cut out some round cherry shims to sit under the shop-made bun feet.

that I made on my lathe. The floor had a slight slope (about $1/4$" over 7'), so the peninsula needed to be raised $1/4$" on the end farthest from the wall. The feet looked great, but I didn't have any way of leveling the island. I was tempted to shave down the feet on the high side of the peninsula, but they were already screwed and glued to its bottom, and it would have been a pain to try and remove them. My solution turned out to be simple. On the band saw, I cut a series of solid cherry discs in varying thicknesses — $1/8$", $3/16$" and $1/4$". They were the same diameter as the feet at the point where they contacted the floor. I was able to slide these custom shims under the feet and voilà, the peninsula was perfectly level and the shims weren't noticeable.

of cabinets, I backed them up against each other and screwed through their backs into the $3/4$" vertical partitions. The end that was exposed was covered with a solid-wood finished panel that was made to match the cabinet doors. The end that butted against the wall was secured with Tapcon masonry fasteners because it was originally an exterior brick wall.

The challenge with this peninsula design revolved around the fact that it was elevated on raised cherry feet

This project focused on using beautiful wood with a natural finish to make its major visual statement, so I didn't go overboard on trim. I installed a thin, light rail to the bottoms of the cabinets and mirrored it at the top with an identical cap molding. This simple and symmetrical treatment provided just the right amount of detail. I used construction adhesive and brad nails to affix the moldings. The moldings come out ¾" from the cabinets so their front edges align with the faces of the cabinet doors. I needed to install a filler strip on the right-hand side of the long run of cabinetry.

Most kitchens use 35mm European-style hinges because they are concealed and provide lots of adjustment. I am a big fan. By turning the screws on the hinges, you can move the door up-and-down, side-to-side and front-to-back. The doors, once adjusted, had nice even reveals with the light rail, the cap molding and each other.

STEP 23 ■ The cabinets were trimmed with a simple, light rail which hides the under-cabinet lights.

STEP 24 ■ The light rail was echoed by an identical trim piece at the top of the cabinets.

STEP 25 ■ I needed to scribe a filler strip at the end of one of the cabinet runs. This creates a neat transition between the wall and the cabinetry.

We used the same door and hardware styles on the peninsula as we did elsewhere in the kitchen, but to make it stand out, we decided to situate the peninsula on a set of turned cherry feet instead of a standard rectangular base. It's also practical to have a small prep sink on the corner where it is next to the cooktop and right across from the refrigerator.

deluxe bathroom

THIS BATHROOM was in such bad shape that we had no where to go but up. The bathroom layout posed some challenges because of a sloping ceiling on one side that had to be factored into our planning. We ultimately decided to move the sink to the left-hand side of the wall to provide more head-room, even though it necessitated extending the plumbing.

In addition to relocating the sink, which required a new vanity, we decided to add two large cabinets. Not only did this provide more storage space, but it looked great. An entire wall of walnut cabinets is a guaranteed resale-value enhancer. The storage cabinets are located beneath the sloped ceiling bump-out, which was tricky to deal with, although I worked out a fairly simple and effective solution. To begin, I ran the cabinets up to the point where the ceiling began to angle out and I capped off the left-hand side with an end cap. I then built and attached cabinet doors that spanned the entire height, so the transition appears seamless from the exterior. I also built a countertop on site from some left-over glass tile that the homeowners had kept from another remodeling project.

This old bathroom was in dire need of a facelift. To accommodate the new vanity, we needed to extend the drain and the water supply lines and move an electric outlet.

CONSTRUCTION STEPS

Once I've developed a general layout for the bathroom, I can plan how I'll build the individual cabinets. This result is the creation of a cutting list which shows me, on one sheet of paper, the dimensions of all the various parts that I'll need. I do this even for simple projects that consist of only one unit, but it is even more critical on larger and more complex projects. Once I've got a cutting list in-hand, it is easy to head to the table saw and start cutting things out. Because I work alone, I had to develop a few strategies for handling sheet goods safely and efficiently. One key to this was to incorporate a rolling cart to help support large panels as they pass over the table saw.

Because I build almost exclusively European-style frameless cabinetry, I needed to apply edge banding to the exposed edges of the plywood and MDF panels that I was using. Real wood edge banding is available in almost every species, and it usually can be applied with an iron. The only tricky part about working with edge-banding is trimming off the excess, because it can tend to snag or

bathroom ceiling bump out — handling a tricky job site challenge

One of the defining characteristics of this site was the sloped ceiling that protruded into the spot where I hoped to place a row of cabinets. To make matters worse, the drywall angled out in both planes. That is to say the ceiling sloped down from front-to-back and left-to-right. If it had only sloped one way, I wouldn't have been so intimidated. Figuring out how to handle the compound slope was a head-scratcher. I initially thought I might have to build some templates, make angled scribe cuts and then patch with a horizontal panel (also angled). Then I realized I could solve the problem by avoiding it.

My solution was simple and I couldn't come up with a reason not to do it. It also allowed me to take advantage of every inch of storage space. I decided to mount an end panel to the left-hand side of the cabinet and stop it before it hit the ceiling bump out. Then I would trim the cabinet doors so they finished at the same height. By measuring up the front of the cabinet to the point where the doors would contact the sloped bump out, I was able to figure the length of the end panel — it would end at the same place as the doors. This process resulted in a cabinet which is open for a few inches on the left side near the top, but I didn't see a disadvantage to this. It was an easy way to solve an otherwise tricky problem.

handling 4×8 sheet goods by yourself

I handle a lot of sheets goods on a daily basis, and I almost always work alone, so I've come up with some strategies that allow me to work safely and with a minimum of hassle.

1. Handle the materials as little as possible. This may sounds obvious but I shudder when I think back to how inefficient I used to be. Nowadays, if I need to cut up to 10 sheets of ³/₄" melamine-covered particle board, I like to buy them on the day that I plan to cut them so I can take them directly from the van to the saw — no unnecessary unloading and stacking. This also helps prevent chipped edges and other collateral damage. I slide them directly from the van onto a cart, which I then push to the table saw for ripping. The sheets remain horizontal the whole time and I never have to lift them. Once the sheets have been cut once, they are more manageable. This approach requires planning your workflow in advance, but is it worth it! This obvious solution took me about seven years to figure out.

2. If you need to bring the materials into the shop and store them for a while prior to the initial cutting, a cart can be a life-saver. If you don't have a cart (mine cost $30 at Target, and, it happens to be the same height as my table saw top), I suggest setting the leading edge of the sheet on the front edge of the saw, then setting the rear edge on the floor. When you're ready, you pick up the rear edge and the table saw top will bear most of the weight of the sheet. You can then cut it as usual. You'll want to make sure that the fence has already been set to the desired width, and, that you have plenty of stable outfeed support. It goes without saying that the table saw should be positioned in a location that is close to the door where the material enters your shop.

I saw a cart distributed by Woodworker's Supply (priced around $250) that can flip vertically stacked panels to horizontal. The cart then provides a steady support so you can feed the panels onto machines or benches as required. I haven't tried it yet, but it looks like a civilized approach.

STEP 1 ■ To safely and easily rip the sheet goods that I used in building these cabinets, I bought a small rolling cart that happened to be the same height as my table saw. Thirty dollars well spent!

STEP 2 ■ Many of the components in this project needed to have their edges covered with iron-on edge-banding.

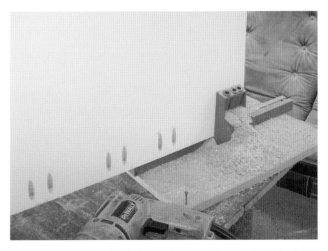

STEP 3 ■ I used pocket holes and screws for much of the joinery in this project.

tear off unevenly, but I recently discovered the best edge-banding trimmer of all time. I haven't had a bad result since then.

I started assembling the vanity cabinet first. The right-hand side of the vanity is exposed, so I had to use a joinery method that would keep the fasteners hidden. I used pocket screws which I concealed on the underside of the cabinet bottom. Biscuits or dominos would've been a fine choice, too. On the left-hand side of the cabinet, I screwed directly through the side panel because the screws will be hidden against the wall.

The back was glued and nailed into place because the area where it joins the side panels won't be visible from the outside. It will be up concealed by the wall on one side and another cabinet on the other. If this area were going to be visible, I would have had to either cut a groove into the cabinet sides and bottom to receive the back, or cover the visible area with a piece of trim.

I usually make my cabinet bases from scrap plywood. This has less to do with economy (although let's face it, it's a factor) than with my great desire to use up my piles

STEP 4 ■ Through-screws provide a strong and fast way of assembling components.

STEP 5 ■ The back of the vanity was nailed on because its edge would be covered by another cabinet.

STEP 6 ■ I use up a lot of scraps when I build cabinet bases. They will be covered by toe-kick trim, so as long as they are sturdy, the material that you use isn't important.

STEP 7 ■ When I need to drill a lot of holes for 35mm hinges, I save time by using my drill press.

STEP 8 ■ These 35mm hinges have a good range of adjustment built-in that helps the installation go smoothly.

and piles of perfectly good scraps. As a result, the parts may not always match, but they will be covered up by toe-kick trim or other components, so it is not a problem.

This modern design calls for doors made from $^3/_4$"-thick plywood panels. To drill the 35mm holes for the hinges, I used a drill press equipped with a fence to ensure consistency. In terms of their vertical placement on the door, the hinges can be positioned anyplace where they won't hit a shelf or cabinet component, but they do need to be centered at 25mm from the edge of the door. If you haven't used European-style hinges before, I recommend practicing on some scrap. I always do a test piece whenever I'm using a new hinge configuration. This helps ensure that my doors will operate properly before I drill the holes in the finished components. The hinges are screwed into the door and the mounting plates are secured to the cabinet sides. I do this in the shop to make sure they will work correctly before I get to the job site. It also saves a bit of time, which fits into my golden rule of doing as much work as I can in the shop.

STEP 9 ■ I always like to set things up in the shop before the installation so I can make sure I've gotten it right.

STEP 10 ■ To level the cabinet bases, I drew a level line on the back wall and set the bases in place. I measured down from the line to the tops of the bases and recorded the measurements at approximately 12" intervals. Comparing these measurements showed me where the floored was out of level. I shimmed the low spots until the measurements showed equal numbers.

plumbing considerations

We were able to lay out the cabinets where we had hoped to, but one practical consideration could have derailed our plans. Our local building code requires the PVC drain line to slope downward ¼" for every horizontal foot that it travels. In this case, the drain line was about six feet long, so it needed to slope at least 1½" over its length. Over the six-foot run, our 2"-diameter pipe occupied nearly all of the available vertical space inside the cabinet base. A longer run of cabinets would not have provided enough height for a consequently longer drain line. We would have needed to relocate the vanity or run the drain line through the cabinets, which would have looked awkward at best. We got lucky, but it demonstrates how the job site can offer obstacles when you least expect them.

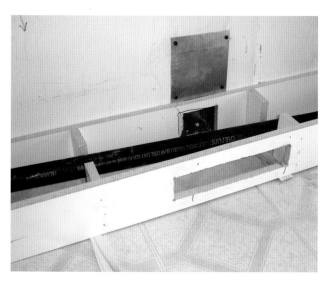

STEP 11 ■ You can see that I need to make a couple of cutouts in one of the bases to accommodate a heat vent. I also had to lay in the sink drain.

The tall storage cabinets were built the same way, except shelf-pin holes needed to be drilled inside the cabinets to accept shelf-pegs for the adjustable shelves..

INSTALLATION STEPS

As is often the case, there was a bit of prep work to do on the job site before the actual installation could begin. In this case, the plumbing lines and an electrical outlet had to be moved. Once these modifications had been made, and the area had been swept out, I was ready to install the cabinet bases.

I began by setting the cabinet bases into their approximate locations and used my level to project a reference line on the wall above the bases. The exact height of the line didn't matter, because I wasn't worried about keeping the cabinets at a particular height. I simply chose a convenient working height.

STEP 12 ■ To make the cutouts in the bottom of the vanity for the drain and supply lines, I measured the size of the lines and their location.

STEP 13 ■ I transferred these measurements to the vanity.

I measured down from the line to the tops of the cabinet bases and made a note of the distance. I repeated this procedure every 12" or so across the entire run of the bases. The goal is to obtain some data about where the floor is or isn't out of level. By comparing the measurements, you can determine which points are lower or higher. The smallest measurement corresponds to the highest point of the floor, and the higher numbers indicate lower spots in the floor. The lowers spots need to be shimmed up until the new measurements are the same as the smallest measurement on the whole span.

In this case, the numbers varied as much as $1/4$", so I shimmed the low spots up until the bases were level. I also needed to make some cutouts for the sink drain and heat vent. Once the bases were shimmed up and the necessary cutouts were completed, I screwed the bases together and then screwed the entire assembly to the studs in the back wall. I used my level to ensure that the bases were also level from front-to-back.

With the bases set, I turned my attention to the cabinets. I installed the vanity first because it was the most complicated. The rest of the process would be easier once it was in place.

The next step was to measure where the sink drain and supply lines were located. I measured from the side wall to the center of the sink drain and from the back. I transferred these measurements to the cabinet bottom. In an effort to do a neat job and remove as little material as possible, I used a $2^1/2$" hole saw. This size hole didn't offer a lot of wiggle room, so I double and triple checked this

Tip: **Codes**

This remodel required a few changes on site before the cabinets could be installed. An electrical outlet needed to be moved, the plumbing supply lines for the drain needed to be extended and a heating vent opening needed to be modified. If your projects require forays into these areas, make sure to familiarize yourself with local building codes and call in the pros as needed.

STEP 14 ■ A hole saw made quick work of drilling the holes.

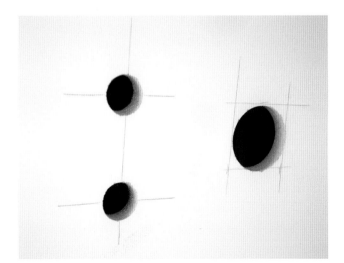

STEP 15 ■ To avoid having a lot of tearout while drilling these holes, I stop drilling when the pilot bit popped through the far side of the material. I resumed drilling from the opposite side.

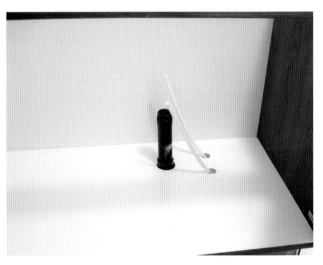

STEP 16 ■ A nice fit.

STEP 17 ■ The cabinet to the right of the vanity got its exposed end capped with a walnut panel.

STEP 18 ■ I secured the panel by screwing through both the vanity and the tall cabinet.

STEP 19 ■ I screwed from the inside of the tall cabinet into the vanity to secure the bottom. Note the shims used to ensure the bottoms of the cabinets lined up.

STEP 20 ■ The cabinets were screwed to studs in the wall.

cut to be sure. The hole location was marked on the outside of the cabinet, so I started drilling from that side, but I switched to the inside before I was done. This prevented the edges of the hole from getting torn up. When the centering bit broke through the other side of the panel I made the switch.

The supply lines were made of Pex tubing (instead of copper tubing), which is somewhat flexible, so there was some wiggle room in deciding where they would enter the cabinet. I drilled a couple of neat holes with a spade bit in a convenient spot and the cabinet dropped nicely into place. I screwed it to the studs in the back wall and moved on.

The tall cabinet next to the vanity needed to have its exposed side finished with a walnut end panel. The back wall was flat, so the back edge of the panel didn't need to be scribed to fit, which saved some time. I secured the panel to the tall cabinet with a number of screws driven from the inside of the cabinet. I also screwed the tall cabinet to the vanity cabinet. I then set the remaining cabinet in place, and, making sure that their front edges were flush, screwed it to the other tall cabinet. Once the cabinets were screwed to each other, I secured them to the wall by attaching them to the studs.

MAKING A GLASS MOSAIC TILE COUNTERTOP ON SITE

This process is the same whether you do it on or off site. Doing it on site made it easy to get a perfect fit.

To get things rolling, I made a subtop from $^3/_4$" plywood and attached it to the cabinet with nails and construction adhesive. I placed the sink on the subtop upside down so that I could position it correctly. This is an aesthetic concern, but it can have practical ramifications. I wanted to make sure I left enough room at the back so I would be able to access the plumbing connections from below. I centered it from side-to-side, but not front-to-back because this would have looked awkward. Instead, I chose a location that looked nice and seemed practical and marked this position on the subtop.

All new sinks come with a template that has cutting dimensions. I aligned this template with the marks on my subtop and traced it. After cutting along the line with my jigsaw, I was able to drop the sink in for a perfect fit.

With the sink removed, I began to position the tiles around the sink cutout. Mosaic tile makes this process easy. You cut the backing with scissors or a knife — no tile saw required. Because I was using a drop-in sink (as compared to an undermount), the tiles didn't need to follow the edges of the cutout exactly, they just needed to be close enough to be covered -by the flanged edge of the sink. You can see that my spacing wasn't quite right. I misjudged how much of the countertop that the sink

STEP 21 ■ To make the tile countertop, I fastened plywood to the top of the vanity with screws and construction adhesive.

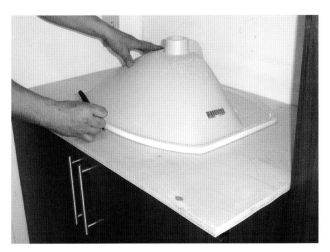

STEP 22 ■ I placed the sink upside down on the plywood to get a feel for where it should be positioned — for both aesthetic and practical reasons.

glass tile countertop

This material is at home anywhere you use ceramic tile. I used it to make some beautiful backsplashes in a kitchen, and I have made a couple of bathroom shower enclosures with it. As long as you seal the grout, it is a low-maintenance product.

Practically speaking, glass mosaic tile is user-friendly material to work with because there is a high likelihood that you won't even have to cut any tile. This saves time and mess and it eliminates the need to rent or buy a pricey tile saw. The tiles come in sheets that measure about 16"×16". You can cut the mesh backing with scissors or a utility knife. Even the curved sink in this bathroom

didn't pose a problem because the rim of the drop-in sink covered an area about 1" beyond the cutout on the countertop. I laid out the tiles for this top in about 5 minutes.

The drawback to this material is cost: glass mosaic tile is expensive — unless you know where to look. I have had terrific experiences with Hakatai (www.hakatai.com), a California-based company with a Web site that includes a custom tile-blend utility that allows you to make your own custom color blends online. They sell for $6-8 per square foot, compared to $20-30 at the tile stores I visited. You can order samples and their customer service is great.

would cover up. This was easy to fix — I cut out three more tiles and set them in place to patch the blank spot.

To adhere the tiles without disturbing my carefully planned layout, I worked in sections. This meant removing small areas of tile and using a notched trowel, according to the mortar manufacturer, to spread mortar little by little. I was then able to press the tiles back on that area and continue with an adjoining area. This shortcut allowed me to work both quickly and accurately. I had some time to kill while the mortar was drying so I put up the mirror. It

was adhered directly to the wall with Mastic mirror adhesive. A big mirror like this helps to give the room a larger look and feel.

Putting up the mirror didn't take long, so I then worked on some of the trim. To install the toe-kick trim, I had to cut around the heating vent opening, which I did by marking the location of the opening on the back side of the trim. To layout the top and bottom of the cutout, I used a tape measure and measured up from the floor. The outside corner of the toe-kick trim was mitered so no end grain

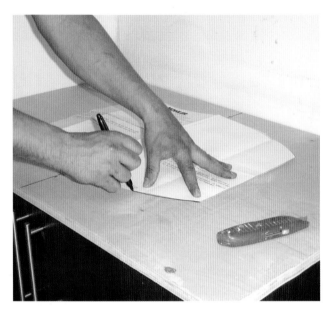

STEP 23 ■ Once I knew where I wanted the sink, I used the template to mark for the cutout.

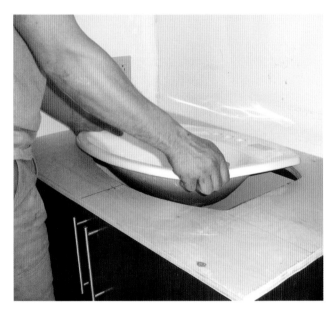

STEP 24 ■ A test-fit confirmed a good fit.

STEP 25 ■ I began laying out the sheets of glass tile and cutting them to fit as needed.

STEP 26 ■ Because the sink overlapped the finished surface by almost $3/4$", it covered up the area at the edge of the cutout, so I didn't need to cut any tiles.

STEP 27 ■ My layout looks good so far.

STEP 28 ■ Dry-fitting the sink showed that I had misjudged the amount of tile necessary to fill in along the back edge. Adding a couple of tiles took care of it.

Tip: **Mortar**

Because this countertop uses a relatively small amount of tile, I used premixed mortar instead of the powdered mix-it-yourself variety. It costs more, nearly twice the price, but this amounted to a $4 cost difference and it saved me time and mess not having to mix it myself. I hated to pay more than the cheapest unit price, but the convenience was a real plus. And, I didn't need an open bag of mortar mix sitting around waiting for another project that may never come down the pike.

STEP 29 ■ To preserve my layout, I removed small sections of tile at a time while I spread the adhesive. This worked well.

STEP 30 ■ Working one section at a time didn't set any speed records but it kept my initial layout intact.

showed. The two pieces appeared to flow together. This is a relatively easy procedure, but I've seen instances where people haven't taken the time to do it and it doesn't look as refined. The vent cover popped in and finished off the toe kick nicely. The travertine floor tiles that were installed later simply butted up against the toe kick, so I didn't need to worry about scribing the bottom edge of the toe kick to the floor.

When the mortar had set up completely, I finished the countertop. The grout was mixed according to the manufacturer's specs. These glass tiles called for unsanded grout. I used a rubber float to trowel the grout on the tiles

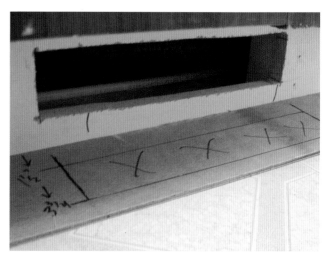

STEP 31 ■ While I was waiting for the tile adhesive to dry, I decided to put up the mirror.

STEP 32 ■ The toe kick trim had to be carefully marked and cut around the heat vent.

STEP 33 ▪ I mitered the corner of the toe-kick trim to create a nice, refined look.

STEP 34 ▪ Once the adhesive had set, I was ready to grout the countertop. I used a rubber float to force the grout between the tiles.

STEP 35 ▪ After the grout had stiffened up, I used a damp sponge to wipe the grout off the countertop.

STEP 36 ▪ I trimmed the exposed edges of the countertop with solid-walnut edging.

and allowed the grout to haze over before being removing it from the surface of the tiles. This takes about fifteen minutes, but it depends on temperature, humidity and how thickly you mixed the grout.

Using a sponge and a bucket of clean water, the grout can be gently wiped off the tiles. This requires frequent changes of water. The rule of thumb says that you're finished when the dirty sponge doesn't cloud up the water when it is placed back in the bucket after wiping the

countertop. For a countertop of this size this was a quick and enjoyable process. I have done larger projects, for instance shower enclosures, and the fun wears off early on and it turns into plain old work.

I glued and nailed the walnut edging in place after grouting because it kept the edging from getting grout slopped all over it, but you could install it beforehand if you're so inclined. In either case, a miter joint makes a nice, neat corner.

sustainable design

I do try to put my money where my mouth is! Going Green is a gradual process, for sure, and I still have a long way to go, but every little bit helps.

This entertainment center was built from bamboo — hot stuff these days as far as Green products go. The cabinet interior was made with formaldehyde-free, melamine-coated particleboard.

It seems like I hear more and more about sustainable *Green* design every day. What was a fringe topic a few years ago has gone mainstream, and there are more opportunities than ever for our projects to incorporate some Green elements. Not surprisingly, there are a few different philosophies and approaches to this subject, so it is worth taking a minute to frame the issues.

On one end of the continuum, the most environmentally-friendly option may be to simply do nothing at all. This doesn't send any waste materials to a landfill, it doesn't put any troublesome chemical compounds into the atmosphere, it doesn't use up any additional natural resources and it avoids the potential health risks associated with certain finishes or adhesives. On the downside, it doesn't result in anything getting done, which probably runs counter to the reason you're reading this book in the first place. So, it may be that the most realistic approach is to recognize the fact that any project will have some environmental consequences but trying to reduce these impacts can make a positive difference nonetheless.

REDUCE, RE-USE RECYCLE — AND GET INFORMED ABOUT YOUR MATERIAL CHOICES

The *three-R* mantra is at the heart of thinking Green. You may have a lot more options than you think in terms of the materials you'll use.

REDUCE

Starting with the first *R*, one of the most obvious strategies is to build smaller and better projects — you'll use less materials and resources. Unfortunately there is a lot of hypocrisy floating around under the shadow of Green design — what my interior designer friend Patrick calls *Greenwashing*. He has a lot of clients who build 10,000+ square-foot vacation homes, install a bamboo floor and pat themselves on the back for being so environmentally friendly. Strange but true. I'm not advocating a spartan, go-without lifestyle for any of us, but separating needs from wants may be a useful part of the planning process.

This kitchen cabinetry was built with melamine-coated wheatboard (a composite board made entirely from wheat). Great stuff!

RE-USE

The *re-use* option may or may not work for you, but again, you may have more options than you think. Every year I do a couple of kitchen re-facings and it always amazes me to see how quickly and easily an entire room can be reshaped by just re-using the cabinets that are already there. If things are in good shape, it makes a lot of sense to just re-clad them with new doors and trim, not only is it environmentally friendly, but it is cheaper, quicker and easier than tearing out a whole run of cabinets and replacing them. And, if you do decide to tear out old cabinets, check around because you may find a non-profit organization in your area that will be thrilled to take your old building materials for re-sale. When I lived in Madison, Wisconsin, I used to make weekly trips to the local Habitat for Humanity resale shop. Not only did they welcome my unwanted stuff, but I found a lot of bargains that made their way home with me.

RECYCLE

It is easy to find materials with *recycled* content these days. For painted projects, I love to use MDF, which is often available with 100% recycled content. A number of companies use formaldehyde-free adhesives to help preserve indoor air quality and reduce greenhouse gases. Particleboard, while not always a first choice for premium woodworking projects, is a great substrate for laminate countertops, and it is usually available with recycled content.

I've also had some great finds at my local architectural salvage yard. Many areas have salvage yards where you can buy cabinets, doors, windows, flooring, lumber and who-knows-what-else at reasonable prices. A little imagination will go a long way towards giving new life to perfectly sound old components.

And, no matter how carefully I plan, every project I create does generate some scraps. Fortunately, my own natural thrift helps me to capitalize on this, and every other woodworker I've ever met seems to fall into the same pattern of hoarding odds and ends to use "someday". I recently built a large shed behind my shop for the sole purpose of storing scrap wood because I got to the point where I didn't have enough space in my shop to warehouse the mountains of scraps that I couldn't bring myself to throw away. This may not be necessary for most folks, but the concept applies — we all love to get the most out of the wood we spend our hard-earned dollars on.

These photos, courtesy of Cabinetpak Kitchens (cabinetpak. com) highlight how refacing cabinets is a cost effective and ecologically sound idea.

SUSTAINABLE FINISHES

As I mentioned early, I don't think it is possible to eliminate our environmental impact all of the time, but if we all make some steps in this direction, the effects will add up to our collective benefit. Quite often, environmentally sustainable approaches and products can be easily integrated into a project without costing more or requiring any additional effort. A great example of this is the use of low-VOC paints and finishing products: even the big-box home centers carry complete lines of low-VOC paints that work just as well as the traditional paints that we're all used to, and the cost difference is negligible. Taking a minute to read the labels is all it takes to make the right choice.

Paints and finishes are great because they not only have the value of being less environmentally harmful, but they also provide some immediate benefits: They are more pleasurable to work with! The no-VOC paints by Olympic (available at Lowe's) have no discernible odor (to me, at least) and they dry quickly so you can recoat rapidly and get your projects done more quickly. They can be custom tinted like regular paints so you can paint with any color you'd like. Olympic also makes my favorite water-based polyurethane — and I've tried a lot of different brands. It is easy to work with and it provides a great finish.

For applying laminates, I like to use water-based contact cements (available at most home centers) because they are easier on the nose and they work just as well as solvent-based contact cements. On some of my projects, I collaborate with a couple of artisans in my area who specialize in interior concrete work. They are able to fabricate refined interior elements such as countertops, fireplace mantles, shower enclosures and more. Their products are considered quite sustainable as they are composed of local components, use natural sealers instead of toxic chemicals and their products are installed close to where they're built. Which brings me to an important issue in sustainable building: Distance. It is easy to get excited about the Green attributes of a particular product, but when it has to be shipped from a few thousand miles away on a pertroleum-burning ship or train, it loses its appeal. So, a local-first mindset may make the most sense. Sometimes you may not have a

Habitat for Humanity ReStores sell donated supplies, new and used, to raise money for the local Habitat affiliate. The community benefits by having access to affordable building and decorating supplies, some of which might otherwise have been thrown away.

Pictured is the Habitat ReStore in Detroit, Michigan.
Photo Credit: HFHI /Steffan Hacker

The Habitat for Humanity ReStores include items that you may not expect to find. Each store is different and the stock will vary accordingly.

Pictured is the Habitat ReStore in Austin, Texas
Photo Credit: HFHI /Steffan Hacker

This center Island (above) and corner TV cabinet were both built using reclaimed lumber removed from the age-old homes and barns throughout New England. Staples Cabinet Makers (staplescabinetmakers.com) uses this lumber to create beautiful pieces of furniture. A great use of what others would see as trash.

The bases used in the Kitchen project were a double benefit. The material was melamine-clad wheatboard, an easily sustainable product, and the pieces were cut from waste pieces from other projects.

choice, but as with all of these issues, being mindful of it will, in the grand scheme of things, make a difference that we'll all be able to appreciate.

My final tip for sustainability in the woodshop is a fun one — tracking down local timber suppliers. And I don't mean big wholesalers who get their lumber shipped in from across the country. I mean the small-timers who have a band-saw mill out back and can tell you right where a given stack of lumber came from. Your access to lumber will depend greatly on where you live. I grew up in upstate New York, and then in Madison, Wisconsin for a few years after that. I was never more than 30 minutes away from small sawmills where I could buy great hardwood lumber (almost always at bargain prices) that was sustainably harvested in the area. Now that I live in Utah, hardwood forests are fewer and farther between, so I don't have the same kind of access that I was used to, but I've found a local arborist who saws up a lot of hardwood lumber which he kiln dries and sells at very reasonable prices. He often stocks semi-exotic species that I wouldn't otherwise have access to (ever use mulberry lumber? My sister now has a dining room table made out of it.). I have even had people call me to say that they were having a tree removed from their yard and it was mine if I wanted it. Three times this has yielded shocking amounts of beautiful hardwood lumber that I had sawn up for pennies on the dollar compared to what I would have normally paid. You might consider placing free classified ads in your area to see if you can find someone who will saw the logs you'll bring in.

General finishes offer stains and top-coat finishes that are ecologically friendly and easy to use. The finishes are available at woodcraft.com and a number of other retail locations.

About five years ago, I was given several fine logs from an ash tree that had to be taken down in my neighborhood. With the help of some friends, I loaded them into my pick-up and took them to a sawmill about 30 minutes away, where I got them sawn into 4/4, 6/4 and 8/4 lumber. I sticker-stacked the boards behind my shop for a couple of years and then began to bring them in for use in all kinds of projects. The sawing cost me about $200 and I got over 1000 board feet of lumber. Some of the planks were almost 20" wide. These three boards went into a tabletop that now has a home about half a mile from where the tree spent its first fifty years —can't get much more local than that.

built-in furniture gallery

Built-in furniture can be installed just about anywhere to enhance the look and feel of a room.

HOYT PLACE BUILT-IN

This built-in is located next to the kitchen (which I also built), and, using the same materials and finish in this adjacent area helped give the impression that the kitchen is larger than it really is. Its symmetrical, rectilinear design creates an ordered feeling — and the large amount of storage came in handy. By lowering the upper unit in the center, we created what, I think, is a more delicate and interesting composition than it would have been had we simply extended that cabinet to the ceiling.

LOEWEN LIBRARY

In ten years of business, I've only fallen in love with two homes that I've worked in. This was one of them — a classic Victorian with all kinds of ornate period details. My client requested a built-in library that would look original. We received the ultimate compliment when the finished product was inspected by a crew of interior designers who thanked him for keeping the original library rather than replacing it with something more modern! The only vintage pieces, however, were the fireplace columns, which I capped with the same built-up crown moulding that I used throughout the room. The use of rope mouldings, frame-and-panel construction techniques and 8"-high baseboards also contributed to the old-world feel of the project.

LAUNDRY-ROOM/OFFICE

This room used to be a run-down mudroom but with a few simple and inexpensive renovations, it was turned into a double-purpose laundry room and office that is a pleasure to spend time in. The countertop is metal-looking laminate installed over particle board with a 2" solid cherry edge and the cabinetry is made from 4/4 cherry and 3/4" cherry plywood. The countertop was set out about 1 1/2" from the wall so cords could be dropped down out of sight. I built a couple of finished panels to go below the countertop (about 6" out from the back wall) to hide both the cords and the plumbing. A major space savings was achieved by purchasing an energy-efficient washer/dryer combo: My understanding is that this technology has been used in Europe for decades but is still new in the United States.

BENHAM OFFICE NOOK

Another perfect opportunity for a built-in existed right across from a butler's pantry. I built a small home-office area which fit neatly below the window, and, we were able to pack a lot of good storage and a useful worksurface into a small area. The trick here was in fitting everything into the enclosed nook: The cabinets dropped in easily enough, but I had to build out the area on the right-hand side to support the solo drawer and to provide a place to anchor the countertop. This was straightforward, but it needed to be done on-site to ensure a perfect fit.

BENHAM BUTLER PANTRY

I built and installed this kitchen last summer and the homeowner decided to capitalize on some ancillary space while we were at it. This niche was situated between the kitchen and the dining room and it proved to be the perfect place for a butler's pantry. The cabinetry extended from wall-to-wall, which required filler strips on each side. To provide both a unique visual element and a practical storage solution, I integrated a custom wine rack into the base cabinetry.

JOHNSON MANTLE AND BOOKCASE

This solid-cherry mantle replaced a dated, bleached-oak mantle which lent no character to the room. I built the new one in one piece, which was feasible because it was narrow and light-weight. This made it easy to deliver and install. I used a French cleat at the back so the new mantle pressed against the wall and slid down into place. Construction adhesive kept it secure. The bookcase was built to be free-standing so it could be moved at the owner's whim.

KAWAKAMI STAIR-UNIT

I've seen a few variations on this idea, but this was my first chance to build one myself, and it turned out great. The cabinets and drawers are deep (36") so we could take advantage of all the space below the stairs, and, the overall design allowed for a nice mix of display and concealed storage. The installation was simple: I built the cabinets about 1" smaller than the space so that they could be shimmed as needed to make everything plumb across the front face. Once the cabinets were secured in place, I ran a couple of trim pieces around the edge of the unit.

suppliers

useful websites, books and other resources

ADAMS WOOD PRODUCTS
423-587-2942
www.adamswoodproducts.com
Wood supply

CLASSIC DESIGNS BY MATTHEW BURAK
800-843-7405
www.tablelegs.com
Wood, wood parts

COLUMBIA FOREST PRODUCTS
www.columbiaforestproducts.com
Wood, hardware, tools, books

**CONSTANTINE'S WOOD CENTER
OF FLORIDA**
800-443-9667
www.constantines.com
Tools, woods, veneers, hardware

FESTOOL
888-550-6425
www.festoolusa.com
Festool Domino Joiner

FRANK PAXTON LUMBER COMPANY
www.paxtonwood.com
Wood, hardware, tools, books

HAKATAI GLASS TILE
888-667-2429
www.hakatai.com
Wood, hardware, tools, books

HIPURFORMER GLUE
800-347-5483
www.titebond.com
Wood, hardware, tools, books

THE HOME DEPOT
800-430-3376 (U.S.)
800-628-0525 (Canada)
www.homedepot.com
*Woodworking tools, supplies and
hardware*

KLINGSPOR ABRASIVES INC.
800-645-5555
www.klingspor.com
Sandpaper of all kinds

LEE VALLEY TOOLS LTD.
800-871-8158 (U.S.)
800-267-8767 (Canada)
www.leevalley.com
Woodworking tools and hardware

LOWE'S COMPANIES, INC.
800-445-6937
www.lowes.com
*Woodworking tools, supplies and
hardware*

ROCKLER WOODWORKING AND HARDWARE
800-279-4441
www.rockler.com
Woodworking tools, hardware and books

ROSEBURG FOREST PRODUCTS
800-245-1115
www.rfpco.com
Wood, hardware, tools, books

TERAGREN BAMBOO
800-929-6333
www.teragren.com
Bamboo veneers

VAN DYKE'S RESTORER'S HARDWARE
800-787-3355
www.vandykes.com
Hardware and restoration supplies

WOODCRAFT SUPPLY LLC
800-225-1153
www.woodcraft.com
Woodworking hardware

WOODWORKER'S HARDWARE
800-383-0130
www.wwhardware.com
Woodworking hardware

WOODWORKER'S SUPPLY
800-645-9292
http://woodworker.com
*Woodworking tools and accessories,
finishing supplies, books and plans*

ADDITIONAL RESOURCES:
www.woodweb.com
Terrific forums on all topics

www.compoundmiter.com
*Crown molding and trim. Install it
like a pro*

www.fscus.org
Forest Stewardship Council
www.treehugger.com
Treehugger blog

www.paulswoodworking.com
Green practices for the woodshop

www.uwcc.wisc.edu/info/kiln.html
Sustainable Woods Cooperative

www.sustainablewoods.net
Sustainable Woods Network
www.massconcretedesign.com
Mass Concrete Design

index

More great titles from Popular Woodworking!

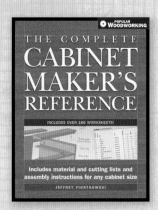

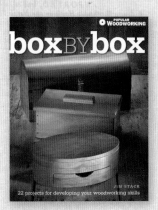

THE COMPLETE CABINETMAKER'S REFERENCE
By Jeffrey Piontkowski

This indispensable resource for cabinetmakers includes cutting and assembly instructions, along with lists of types and quantities of materials needed for all standard-sized cabinets. You'll also learn how to adapt the projects to build custom-sized pieces.

ISBN 13: 978-1-55870-757-3
ISBN 10: 1-55870-757-3
hardcover w/concealed wire-o, 128 p., #70710

BOX BY BOX
By Jim Stack

Hone your woodworking skills one box at a time. In the pages of this book you'll find plans for 21 delightful boxes along with step-by-step instructions for making them. The projects include basic boxes that a novice can make with just a few hand tools to projects that will provide experienced woodworkers with an exciting challenge.

ISBN 13: 978-1-55870-774-0
ISBN 10: 1-55870-774-3
hardcover w/concealed wire-o, 144 p., #70725

GLEN HUEY'S ILLUSTRATED GUIDE TO BUILDING PERIOD FURNITURE
By Glen Huey

Woodworkers will learn to build their own high-end period furniture with clear, concise instructions, step-by-step photos and a bonus DVD ROM of real-time demonstrations and printable plans.

ISBN 13: 978-1-55870-770-2
ISBN 10: 1-55870-770-0
hardcover w/concealed wire-o, 128 p., #70722

These and other great woodworking books are available at your local bookstore, woodworking stores or from online suppliers.

www.popularwoodworking.com

Easy to Use
Compatible with both Mac and PC, the disc contains live-action demonstrations and instructions showing how to set bases, set cabinets and install filler strips. Also, how to make cutouts for plumbing and electric and make a template to aid in the installation of a cabinet top.

BUILT-IN FURNITURE FOR THE HOME

Bonus Disc Table of Contents

Jobsite Strategies You Can Use

introduction
getting started
setting the bases
installing base cabinets
making cutouts
making a template